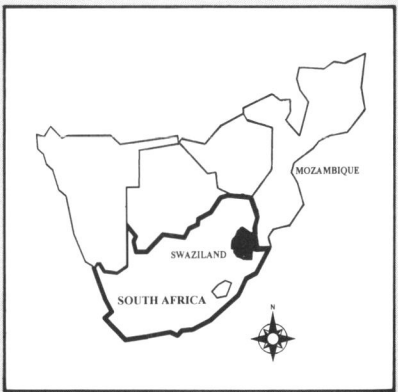

VISITORS' GUIDE TO SWAZILAND

VISITORS' GUIDE TO SWAZILAND

HOW TO GET THERE · WHAT TO SEE · WHERE TO STAY

Marco Turco

SOUTHERN
BOOK PUBLISHERS

This book is fondly dedicated to Jody . . . and with devotion to
Saraswati.
Om Sri Saraswati Namah.

ISBN 1 86812 530 0

First edition, first impression 1994

Published by
Southern Book Publishers (Pty) Ltd
PO Box 3103, Halfway House 1685

Cover photograph by Jody Turco
Maps by Colin Stevenson
Set in 10/11.5 pt Palatino by
Kohler Carton & Print (Natal)
Printed and bound by
Kohler Carton & Print (Natal)

ACKNOWLEDGEMENTS

Without the dedication and assistance of numerous people, both in South Africa and Swaziland, this book would not have reached completion. I offer my gratitude to them.

To Darron Raw, thanks for all the advice, information and concern. The many faxes, telephone calls and pamphlets were invaluable. Your insights, anecdotes and energy were pivotal in the theme of this book.

The Reilly family; your honest kindness and hospitality touched our hearts and eased the pain. Beauty can be difficult to see sometimes.

To my wife Jody; for tolerating all my late nights, bad moods and missed meals. Your support, encouragement and love still amazes me.

Friends and family for the dinners, relaxation and telephone calls. Nicholas, Karen and Cameron, for moments of laughter, ideas and comfort.

Colin, Shanette and Craig Stevenson. Is it just me, or was it really easier this time? The next maps should be a breeze.

The hoteliers and innkeepers who assisted us with times of respite and sanctuary. Not least, the management of the Highland Inn and Mountain Inn.

Michael Litchfield; for your time and effort in providing me with material on Swaziland.

Louise Grantham; for the book, tea and suggestions.

To those many not mentioned by name, I thank you all, the kindness and friendship will never be forgotten.

CONTENTS

INTRODUCTION

Like an emerald in the blondes and grey of southern Africa, Swaziland sparkles as the smallest country in the southern hemisphere. One of the last ruling monarchies in Africa, it reveals a warmth, hospitality and tradition that has virtually disappeared from the continent.

There are a growing number of people who are tired of visiting the usual resorts and following over-utilised trails. For many, there is a search for places that are remote, where life still gently flows at a pace governed by the rhythms of nature. They seek destinations that, while providing tourist class accommodation in certain areas, still offer regions of tribal tradition.

Swaziland is a country where wilderness still means open, unfenced savanna and indigenous forest. Perhaps it is for these reasons that the number of people visiting Swaziland each year is increasing at such a rate.

Swaziland has a multitude of things to offer visitors, such as its nonpareil combination of natural splendour and tribal customs. The creativity of the Swazis is unequalled in Africa. Their handicrafts and art works are unique on the continent.

Sadly, with the arrival of Western advisers, these traditional techniques and designs are being mass produced, with a decrease in intrinsic beauty and creativity.Travelling in Swaziland is easy. Public transport is efficient, crowded and cheap. Fuel is available at every town. And, with the smallness of the country, it is quite possible to see an entire region within a few days. Hiking is not a major drawcard but in the Lebombo mountains and game parks of Swaziland, hikers will find trails, rural accommodation and hospitality a big attraction. Recently, white water rafting on the Lusutfu river has encouraged adventurous visitors to spend a day riding the rapids of Swaziland's largest river.

In preparing for your trip, make certain passports are valid, health certificates have been updated and driving permits ordered. Arrange for travellers cheques and hard currency. If necessary, apply for a visa from the relevant diplomatic mission. Contact hotels, giving exact dates of arrival. Have photocopies made of travellers cheques, passport, identity document and licences. Always useful, take at least four passport-sized photographs. Business cards make cheap but important gifts. Hand them out frequently, especially to chiefs and headmen.

Be prepared for a land of contrasts and paradoxes, where new meets old, and Western culture mixes with African. In Mbabane and the Ezul-wini valley, the contrasts are strikingly obvious. Tourists rush about in airconditioned vehicles, while less than 2 km from the bright lights, men plough fields with oxen and hand ploughs.

For rural people, modernisation in Swaziland does not exist. They remain without electricity, and still walk to collect water from rivers. It is said that Swaziland is a natural history museum – a rich storehouse of vegetation, wildlife, geography and tribal beliefs.

Visitors to whom adventure and the great outdoors are necessary for a vacation, should consider travelling this jewel of wild, tribal Africa. Swaziland is one of the last countries that still provides tourists with a window into the Africa of legend. During ritual ceremonies you will be able to witness traditions that have been followed since the birth of the Bantu-speaking peoples. See it now, before foreign aid, hotel chains and tour operators steal the mystery away forever.

As the population continues to grow, the demand for agricultural land also increases, effectively reducing the wildlife areas. Hlane, Mlil-wane and Mkhaya game sanctuaries are a solution to this problem as the Swazi monarchy realises that its wildlife is an asset which can earn much-needed revenue from tourism. Poachers, however, have a different, short-term, agenda. Slaughter of wildlife has reached alarming proportions. Only with the dedication and commitment of men like Ted Reilly, will Swaziland's greatest asset – her wilderness and wildlife – survive. Pressure is mounting though. Already, in certain districts, what were once mystical chiefdoms have been replaced by huge agricultural corporations. Raping nature of her tranquillity and limited bounty, they reduce the areas that were once attractive to visitors. Before it is too late, go and see the Swaziland of myth and legend.

Many visitors will return saying that Swaziland's beauty touched them in an esoteric way, that their lives have been changed for the better by being among the last vestiges of African tribalism. The spirituality inspired by this wonderful country combines with the serenity of the Swazi people, to create a journey of both body and soul. By spending time with the tribesmen in their remote villages, visitors will learn more about themselves and how to cope with the chaos of the 20th century.

Swaziland's wild places are still Eden. Her people are changing too, but their lives still linger in yesterday. Swaziland can best be summed up in the words of a village chief near Balegane, "We are a happy people. We do not expect too much from others. We just want to continue as our forefathers did. But, we see that change is coming, quickly and violently. Our valleys and kraals are being destroyed by the monster of the west. People must come quickly, to see the vanishing face of Swaziland."

HOW TO USE THIS GUIDE

While it is possible to visit Swaziland without prior planning, the journey will be easier, more pleasant and exciting, if you have some idea of where you are going before departure. Getting a detailed map of the country should be a priority. Then, write or telephone the Swazi Tourist Board or embassy for pamphlets and information about Swaziland.

Chapter 1 provides visitors with introductory facts about the country. Not claiming to be definitive, this information is merely the groundwork for deeper research. Chapter 2 contains useful facts for the visitor. All countries have peculiarities concerning their laws, customs and traditions. Some prior knowledge is highly recommended. Chapters 3 and 4 detail transport to and around Swaziland. From budget traveller to tourist, all will find useful guidelines here. Chapter 5 describes the capital city of Mbabane. Pertinent information, and a map, provide quick, easy and valuable references.

Having decided which area of the country you would like to visit, consult the suggested routes. In Chapter 6, the Ezulwini valley is described with its hotels, casinos and nightlife. Chapter 7 takes travellers on a visit to the agricultural districts in southern Swaziland. Chapter 8 describes the route through Central Swaziland. Finally, chapter 9 explores the remote tribal regions of northern Swaziland.

Put this guide in your pocket. Where you find things different, make a note in the book. Africa is always unpredictable; Swaziland is no exception. If you discover changes that could affect future travellers, please write and tell me. All letters and queries will be answered. Useful information will be retained and used in updated editions.

1 FACTS ABOUT THE COUNTRY

HISTORY AND GOVERNMENT

Swaziland was inhabited by the Khoisan nomads for thousands of years before the settlement of the region by Bantu-speaking clans. In Swaziland there are relics of the early negroid tribes dating back to as early as AD 300. Noted for frequent controversies and arguments, the view held by most anthropologists and archaeologists is that the Bantu tribes entered the southern African region from north of the Limpopo river, possibly from central West Africa.

It was not until the end of the 15th century that the fragmented clans of south-east Africa began to unite into stronger, more cohesive communities. The leader who rose up and started the unification was Chief Dlamini. Concerned about the safety and future of his followers, Dlamini trekked with his people, following the flow of the Komati river into the Lebombo mountains, and then across grasslands to present day Maputo. Nearly 180 years later, under the leadership of Ngwane, the tribe was once again uprooted and moved back across the mountains, this time following the Pongola river valley. After almost four months of travel, Chief Ngwane halted the trek in the forested and tsetse fly free valleys in what is now the Swaziland province of Shiselweni.

Living predominantly pastoral-herding lives, the people prospered in their secluded valleys. In 1780 Ngwane died, and a period of instability followed under the terrifying rule of Ndungunye. Succeeding Ndungunye was King Sobhuza I. A domineering but wise man, he foresaw problems for his fledgling nation. To the south, the mighty Zulu impis under their legendary king, Shaka, were sweeping across the green hills of Zululand claiming land, demanding allegiance and dealing death. Rather than face the awesome armies of Shaka, Sobhuza I decided to move his community further north. Sending out scouts and spies, he soon had enough information on the northern areas to confidently migrate up to the valley of the Lusutfu river. Apart from offering good grazing and water, there were several caves and tunnels in the surrounding hills. These were to be used as shelter should the Zulus attack the new settlements.

Most of the region at that time was inhabited by Tswana and Sotho tribesmen who, being smaller and weaker were soon subjugated by

Sobhuza I. While not intent on building an empire, Sobhuza I was interested in increasing his own people's wealth in the form of confiscated livestock. But, Sobhuza I still had his doubts about the safety of his young nation. So, to guarantee their survival, he invited Shaka to his royal kraal at Lobamba. Shaka, not known for his diplomacy, surprisingly accepted. After several days of feasting, dancing and discussions Shaka returned south with two new wives, daughters of King Sobhuza I, who had been given as gifts. Sobhuza I meanwhile, had the word of Shaka that no harm would befall his people while Shaka ruled.

Shortly after his death in 1839, Sobhuza I was succeeded by his capable and ambitious son, Mswati. It was from Mswati that the Swazi nation took its name. When Mswati ascended the throne, his kingdom was over twice Swaziland's present size. Following the example of the Zulus, Mswati formed regiments and armies from the men under his rule. Never confident enough to break the fragile peace with the Zulus, Mswati turned north and west for his campaigns. But sadly, the descent into temporary subservience had already begun. In his bid to quickly develop the Swazis into a formidable group, Mswati assimilated numerous other tribes into his kingdom. Neither as powerful nor as aggressive as the Swazi, these other tribes on the western, northern and southern frontiers were gradually being pushed back by the advancing white settlers trekking up from the Boer Republics.

Despite the migration north by the white farmers (Boers), it was prospectors who were the first Europeans into the area. Having tried their luck at panning and digging for gold in South Africa, they turned hungry eyes on the undoubtedly mineral-rich hills and mountains of Swaziland. Until his death in 1858, Mswati was adamant in his denial of any extensive land rights to non-Swazis; he did however grant privileged prospectors small-claim titles in 1845. His successors, first Ludonga and shortly thereafter Mbandzeni, were neither as determined, nor as aware of the dangers that an influx of whites would bring to their kingdom. They readily granted concessions to an ever-increasing number of white miners, farmers and traders until their extensive royal holdings had been reduced to Swaziland's present size in 1889 when Mbandzeni died.

Foreigners at this time were moving freely throughout the country, trading from the Kobolondo hills in the west to the majestic escarpment of the Lebombo mountains in the east. To the north, at Pigg's Peak, the famous Devil's Reef was yielding high grade gold that was being transported out of Swaziland and into South Africa. To further entrench their authority, the Transvaal Boer Republic annexed Swaziland as a "dependency." There had been no prior consultation with the new king, Banu. In an attempt to remove the power of the Swazi king, the Boers falsely accused him of murder, and he was forced to flee south, into the territory of the Zulus, for safety. Under Boer rule the Swazi nation suffered terribly; to pay the taxes that the Transvaal Republic had imposed on them, many were forced into virtual slavery as farm and mine labourers.

Following the British victory in the Boer War, Swaziland was inherited by the British Crown as part of the spoils of war. Although unhappy about being loaded with another poor African country to govern, the British sent a High Commissioner to the country in 1906. While under the distant administration of Great Britain, the Swazis were allowed to keep a degree of autonomy. Queen Lomawa claimed royal rights to the throne due to her lineage. She kept a shaky peace with the British until her death in 1921, when her son King Sobhuza II ascended the Swazi throne.

The British however carried out their duties as colonisers and promptly expropriated almost 40 per cent of Swazi land, which they gave out as further concessions to white settlers. By the start of the 1930s most Swazi territory was in the hands of immigrants.

The British method of governing Swaziland prevented any of the locals from owning too much property. What resulted was an almost feudal system of control. Sobhuza II himself was not averse to this system as it removed any threat to his sovereignty from Swazi landowners. In addition, by only allowing the people to rent small tracts of land, the British administration, together with Sobhuza II, were able to demand their rights to annual crops from a much larger number of subjects. Still, no matter how much authority Sobhuza may have had over his Swazi tribesmen, any directive that involved more than three per cent of the nation had to first be cleared with the British colonial administration. Britain never really exerted any dire authoritarian rule over Swaziland, and in 1968 she gave the country back to the Swazi monarchy.

One of the first things Sobhuza II did after independence was to buy back as much of the land and trading concessions as possible. This desire to recapture national identity was to be a trademark of King Sobhuza II's reign. In his bid to return concession land to the Swazi people he was frequently overcharged for the purchases. This spending beyond the newly independent country's budget was to cause considerable economic hardship for a number of years.

Things were soon to get even worse as the expanding middle classes gained further education and began to question the right to be governed by a monarch instead of a parliament. In a desperate attempt to stem the almost revolutionary attitude that seemed prevalent in Swaziland, Sobhuza II imposed a state of emergency and banned all trade unions and affiliated causes.

Little has changed in Swaziland since the death of Sobhuza II in 1982. The choice of a new king was not easy. Sobhuza II was a virile man who, apart from having over 100 recognised wives, had officially fathered in excess of 200 sons, all of whom wanted a "shot" at reigning. At his death there was no immediate replacement for the throne and it was filled by the Queen Regent Dzeliwe (Great She Elephant). Dzeliwe was disliked by many members of the ruling family as well as being unpopular with most Swazis. She was usurped in 1984 by Ntombi, another of Sobhuza II's sizeable harem. Ntombi's son, Prince Makhosetive was recalled from school abroad and became the youngest monarch in Swazi history, King Mswati III in 1986.

The country is still officially a monarchy. The King has executive and legislative authority, as well as symbolic representation of the country. Today there is a National Council consisting of a Cabinet of ministers led by the Prime Minister. Parliament has two houses: the House of Assembly and the Senate House. Under the auspices of the young king, Mswati III, policies and plans are discussed by the ministers, with decisions taken by the king under advisement from his experienced ministers. Nowadays the king's decrees are enacted by a parliamentary vote rather than in an autocratic manner – as was the custom of his father, Sobhuza II. There is however a fair amount of discontent in Swaziland. Many of the academics and intellectuals secretly criticise the aristocracy, but balk at public denouncements – the memory of Sobhuza II's bloody crushing of the workers' parties in 1972 is still a deterrent to the dissatisfied.

Despite the continuing stringent measures taken against rebellious citizens, discontent among the Swazis has on several occasions spilled onto the streets. In 1975, fed up with their poor salaries and treatment, railway workers downed tools and marched on the Royal Kraal at Lombamba to hand a petition to the king. They never achieved their objective; 2 km from the kraal, police and soldiers sprayed the crowd with rubber bullets and tear gas. Many were injured and a group of what were purported to be the ringleaders, were imprisoned.

In 1977, angry at atrocious salaries, poor working conditions and little state assistance, nearly 500 teachers went on strike. Sobhuza's response was to immediately ban the National Teachers Association and dismiss as many of the association's leaders as possible. Students and their parents were shocked at the move, and in sympathy with the dismissed teachers came out in public demonstrations of support early in 1978. Once again, the king opted for retaliation with force. Sending in both police and army, he gave orders to not only disperse the demonstrators but to use any force deemed necessary. The paramilitary forces felt little compassion and their heavy-handed treatment of offenders resulted in citizens rioting and damaging any accessible government property in both Mbabane and Manzini, as well as in the smaller urban centres.

Nothing has changed in the way that discontent or rebelliousness are dealt with. This has led to a number of underground organisations being formed. Most of these organisations aim at removing the monarchy and implementing a more social-democratic form of government. Surprisingly, the majority of members in these movements are professionals and white-collar workers who see beyond the obvious faults of a nobility and want a change in line with current world trends.

Whatever the loyalties of individual Swazis, visitors may be surprised that a country with such a poor standard of education and literacy has such politically aware and active constituents. Be prepared for discussions on politics wherever you stop. Undoubtedly, the best policy is to remain noncommittal whatever your particular allegiance – ultimately the country is theirs and any judgmental opinions you may present could result in an unpleasant and potentially dangerous situation.

Being landlocked, Swaziland has to walk a tightrope of diplomacy. To the east, Mozambique was engaged in a debilitating and economically suicidal civil war for several years. This has made trade with that country almost impossible, meaning that Swaziland has had to rely almost solely on her powerful neighbour, South Africa, for trade. South Africa, fully aware of the position in which Swaziland finds herself, has effectively exploited the situation. On a number of occasions the Swazi military and security forces have been coerced into working with the South African police against alleged African National Congress and Pan-Africanist Congress soldiers hiding in Swaziland.

Swaziland has had little choice but to work with the South Africans whenever requested to – well over 90 per cent of all investment and technical expertise is supplied by the wealthy industries and conglomerates of South Africa. In addition to large-scale South African investment, over 16 000 Swazis work in South Africa. This state of affairs between South Africa and Swaziland is best summed up by travel writer, Geoff Crowther, who wrote in 1989 that South Africa's Big Brother attitude has led to her viewing Swaziland, "as its most successful homeland".

GEOGRAPHY AND CLIMATE

Swaziland has a total area of 17 363 square km. Geographically it is a wonderland for travellers; from plunging waterfalls and sheer mountain cliffs, to wide valleys and sluggishly flowing rivers, it excites and tantalises visitors no matter what their previous travel experience.

There are four distinct regions making up Swaziland: highlands, midlands, lowlands and Lebombo mountains. Along the eastern border is a natural boundary formed by the stumpy Lebombo mountains. This mountain range runs north-south, separating Swaziland from Mozambique and Zululand to the east. Along the western extremities of the country, shielding it from South Africa, are the Kobolondo, Ntababomvu, Makonjwa and Mahlangatsha granite hills of the Swazi highlands. Situated at the juncture of the Kobolondo and Ntababomvu sections is the highest mountain in Swaziland: Emlembe (1 863 m). Between this granite escarpment and the Lebombo mountains are the valleys, rivers, plains and seemingly endless hills that rate Swaziland high among the most beautiful countries on earth.

In the northern reaches of Swaziland travellers will find the tranquil Ponjwane and Muccucene hill ranges; an area of high mist-covered hills, indigenous and exotic forests, and river gorges. Central Swaziland is an amalgam of the highlands and lowlands; an area of folds that results in the chaotic profusion of the Maliaquma hills and Bulunga mountains which fade out into wide alluvial valleys east of Mkhaya Nature Reserve. To the south, steep gorges and plunging valleys muddle their way through the Mahlangatsha and Lugolweni hills to the border with South Africa.

Swaziland is divided into four provinces: in the north-west is the predominantly highland province of Hhohho. Edging the Lebombo mountains to the east is the largest province, Lubombo. The mainly lowland province of Shiselweni is tucked into the small Nkondololo and Mhlosheni hills in the far south; Manzini province encompasses the Mahlangatsha, Mbutini and Bulungu hills and Grand Valley.

With its "crumpled paper" landscape of hills, mountains and valleys, Swaziland is graced with a myriad rivers, streams and waterfalls. The mighty Lusutfu river, which starts as a tiny stream on the high plateau of South Africa's eastern Transvaal, drops down the escarpment in a series of dramatic falls, draining a large area of central Swaziland, and is the main river in the country. The Komati river in the north, flows from South Africa, across Swaziland, back into South Africa and then becomes the Incomati through Mozambique to the sea at Ponta de Macaneta. In the south, the Ngwavuma and Sitilo rivers spill into the Pongola river which flows through Mozambique and empties into the Indian Ocean near Bela Vista as the Maputo river.

Swaziland is so small that weather experienced in one region is also likely to occur throughout the country. Occasionally however, a frontal depression that has drifted across South Africa will only touch the extreme southern regions around Shiselweni province, or veer west and bring the heavy mist which is characteristic of the western highlands.

These isolated weather patterns are rare and visitors can count on the climate being uniform throughout the country. Cocooned between mountains and protected by countless hills and valleys, most of Swaziland is a low-lying hilly country, below the Transvaal highveld plateau. Protected as it is from the bitter winters of the highveld and the high summer humidity of the coastal regions, Swaziland has a climate that is both invigorating and healthy throughout the year.

The change in seasons is seldom immediately obvious, and visitors may find themselves caught unawares by an unexpected thunderstorm or sudden temperature drop. Swaziland does not have the extremes in climatic conditions that are found in Lesotho and in the highlands of South Africa. This is not to say that there are no seasonal variations. Summer's heat first becomes noticeable about September, at the same time that the first of the rains arrive. By the end of October the rainy season has set in, with temperatures continuing to rise until their peak in early February. Be prepared for days of glorious sunshine and evenings of ferocious storms and heavy rain in most areas, especially on the heights of the Lebombo mountains.

At this time it can become very warm in the southern regions of Swaziland, particularly for visitors who have arrived from European countries. Daytime temperatures range between 20°C at dawn to about

32°C at noon. The best escape is to head for the northern hills around Pigg's Peak, where the slightly higher altitude brings some relief with lower night temperatures.

Autumn creeps in from mid-March to mid-April. There is no dramatic change in the plant life, and apart from a few exotic trees near the highest peaks in the Kobolondo and Ntababomvu hills, most of the vegetation remains green until early to mid-winter. Winter is only felt from about June and lasts for a few short weeks until July. In the lower lying provinces winter is barely felt at all, with the vegetation staying green and the thermometer seldom dropping below 24°C at noon. In the Lebombo mountains along the eastern border, and in the highland areas around Pigg's Peak, zero degrees will rarely be reached. Snow is virtually unheard of and winter days are comfortable enough so that no big coats or heavy jerseys are necessary. During winter in the mountain areas however, jerseys are often required at night.

Choosing a time for travel is more dependent on your mode of transport and what you expect to see than a particular season. Wildlife enthusiasts should try to get up into the mist-belt forests and midland regions between September and October. This is when birds are hatching their eggs and game are calving. Hikers exploring the hill and mountain provinces will experience the best hiking weather between August and September. Nature's new growth is just beginning and while the days are pleasant and warm, occasional short, light rains dampen the dust in the late afternoons. Visitors with their own transport or using public transport should avoid travelling between October and December. Most of the annual rain falls during this period and for those intending to visit remote areas the roads can become impassable due to flooding and washaways.

FESTIVALS AND HOLIDAYS

Before the arrival of missionaries bringing Christianity, the inhabitants of the region led lives full of shamanic ritual and spiritual contact. Even today, while Christianity is widespread, the tribal beliefs and traditions are still practised by most Swazi. This has led to a strange but fascinating mixture of ceremonies, holidays and festivities.

Before the arrival of the Nguni people, the Khoisan lived in harmony with their surroundings. Many of their paintings on ancient rock caves look like surreal spacecraft and hint at cosmic relationships and a philosophy that has long disappeared.

After the Khoisan came Bantu-speaking people. With them they brought a younger but no less powerful religion, in the form of ancestor worship (animism).

To the Nguni tribes, as to Hindus of India, the cow was the mother figure of life. She was the compassionate and charitable Mother Divine in the guise of a patient animal. Today, hundreds of years after their arrival in southern Africa, the Nguni people still regard the cow as holy. Marriages of nearly all Swazis involve a transaction in cattle. When a prospective groom pays with cattle (a system known as lobola), it will be with the best of his herd. This payment is not only a way of indicating the wealth of the groom and his family, but is also an important tradition that is still endorsed and practised by most tribal communities throughout Africa.

In Swaziland, the traditional number of cattle paid in marriage is 12 head, with the number rising depending on the lineage of the bride-to-be. When it is time for a king to take a wife however, it becomes a payment made by the Swazi people and all chiefs in the kingdom are expected to contribute cattle for the enormous payment that must be made for a future "Mother of the Nation" .

Animist faiths have always been strong on ceremonies, and although in many countries these traditions are practised secretively and officially banned, Swaziland is refreshingly different. Four ceremonies are officially conducted each year although numerous others occur throughout the year in the more remote districts. These four are: Umhlanga (Reed Dance), Swaziland's most famous celebration, the Ncwala (First Fruits); a time for feasting, politics and worship, Umcwasho; a disciplined military tattoo for warriors, and the most auspicious and ancient, Tinkomo Temadloti; a gathering to honour and renew vows to the ancestors whose spirits are there to assist or destroy.

Apart from being the "first fruits" celebration, the Ncwala is also the time when the king, his princes and chiefs gather for their annual discussions, as well as to declare publicly the unity of the Swazi clans. Until very recently, this celebration was closed to non-Swazi viewing. Today, with a greater degree of leniency extended to foreigners, visitors to Swaziland during the last months of the year should make every effort to attend those parts of the ceremony which are accessible.

The ceremony lasts three weeks, and in that time festivities are held in towns and villages all over Swaziland; each site holding the celebration for two days before it is passed on to a neighbouring village or town. The actual ceremony commences with traditional sacred dances and rituals after sunset on a day about 21 days before the summer solstice on 21 December. On the night the first dances begin, the king rises in front of his subjects and literally spits a liquid potion to the four points of the compass. This act symbolises the unity and absence of duality that exists between the king and the powerful forces of the spirit world. The third day of the ceremony, the Day of the Bull, is a part of the celebration that visitors with weak stomachs should avoid. A black bull is first blessed by the king and then sent into an enclosure where young boys wrestle with, and then publicly slaughter, the terrified creature. Once this first bull has been killed, another black bull is led into the same enclosure. This time however the animal is not slaughtered. Instead the king, who has disrobed – except for a traditional weapon and loin-skin – adopts a pose of dominance over the bull which has been forced onto its knees by warriors. This symbolises the king's potency, virility and bull-like strength.

The Ncwala climaxes at sunset on the 18th day, when the king, dressed in skins and painted with magical paints, descends to dance and mix with his loyal subjects. Due to the potential danger from enemies of the now vulnerable king, most foreigners will be asked to leave the immediate area at this time. At the climax of the ceremony, the king is given a gourd to hold, which is the symbol of the origins of the Nguni peoples. To acknowledge the first tribesmen to the region the king will then point this gourd towards the north: towards Central Africa and the original home of the Swazis' ancestors. Once the gourd rite is over the partying can begin, for now the king has officially proclaimed the start of the Swazi New Year. The following two days are spent in recovering, pensive seclusion and silence, until at sunset on the final day, the king emerges to be seen by his subjects. A final round of spiritual songs and dances is performed to the ancestors, whose blessing and pleasure are hopefully confirmed by a torrential downpour shortly thereafter. There is a great feast to which foreigners, who are usually banned from the climactic events of the 18th day, are invited. This is a wonderful time to be in Swaziland. It gives visitors a chance to mingle with a still tribal people, and feel the strong bonds that tie this nation to the natural and astral realms.

Mixed Christian-animist religions are not the only faiths followed in Swaziland. With a spirit of tolerance, the kings of Swaziland have always allowed freedom of religion. Visitors will find all the great religions of the world represented to some degree in Swaziland. Muslims, Hindus, Christians and a sprinkling of Buddhists all worship as they please in a country that is regarded as the most stable on the African continent. With a present population close to one million people, this lends itself to a fascinating polyglot of cultures, made more expressive by the unified desire for a peaceful, prosperous Swaziland.

There are 12 annual public holidays in Swaziland. Travellers should take note that government offices, banks and most businesses are closed at this time. If possible, avoid doing anything either side of a public holiday that will involve a queue. Not only are there wasted hours of waiting, but there is also the apathy of the clerks to deal with. It is a good idea not to visit any of the larger urban centres on, or near, a public holiday.

Public holidays
New Year's Day – 1 January
Good Friday
Easter Monday
King Mswati III's birthday – 19 April
National Flag Day – 25 April
Ascension Day
Late King Sobhuza II's birthday – 22 July
Reed Dance Day (Umhlanga)
Independence Day (Somhlolo) – 6 September
Ncwala Day
Christmas Day – 25 December
Family or Boxing Day – 26 December

2 FACTS FOR THE VISITOR

VISAS

Swaziland visa regulations have been through a number of changes in the last few years, due to the political turmoil that seems to plague her neighbours, South Africa and Mozambique. All foreigners entering Swaziland, including minors (under 16) who are not registered in their parents' passports, need to have valid passports or travel documents. Only a few countries' citizens require visas. No visa is required for citizens of South Africa, Lesotho, Malawi, Comoros Islands, all Commonwealth countries but excluding Mauritius, India, Sri Lanka (Ceylon) and Bangladesh.

Although passport holders from EEC countries are required to have a visa, they can now forgo the tedium of organising it before their trip, and simply get one at their port of entry. Travellers intending to travel in South Africa, who do not have South African passports, should remember that visas are required for most visitors to that country. Re-entry visas can be obtained for people living in South Africa, but not holding South African passports, from the Department of Home Affairs; Visa and Passport Section, Private Bag X11, Johannesburg, 2000. Tel. (011) 836-3228, fax 834-6623.

If you intend staying longer than 60 days in Swaziland, you will have to apply for a temporary residence permit from the Chief Immigration Officer. To do this in Swaziland involves going through reams of paperwork, idle hours and mountains of officialdom. You will be forced to waste at least a full day on this test of patience. It is a far better idea to apply for a temporary residence permit from outside Swaziland. This can either be done directly through the Chief Immigration Officer, P.O. Box 372, Mbabane, Tel. (International code 09268) 4-2941/6, or more conveniently – if travelling overland across South Africa – from the efficient and helpful Swaziland Trade Mission, postal address: P.O. Box 8030, Johannesburg, 2000. Physical address: 9th Floor, Rand Central Building, 165 Jeppe Street, Jeppe, Johannesburg. Tel. (011) 299776/8, fax 299763.

Beyond the borders of the Southern African Common Customs Area, (South Africa, Namibia, Lesotho, Botswana), Swazi visas are obtainable from Swazi embassies and consular and legation offices, and are relatively cheap in comparison to other African visas. (See section under Consulates and Embassies.) It is advisable to start applying for your visa or temporary residence permit well in advance; you can expect a wait of anything from three to eight weeks for a postal visa, even longer if there are any incorrect or invalid entries on your application form. Make certain to read the application form carefully. Make at least three copies of the form, keeping another three for your travel documentation.

Check that you have requested a multiple-entry visa when making the initial application. Not only does this allow you to pop back and forth between South Africa or Mozambique and Swaziland, it also saves filling in all those forms again.

Do not be surprised if your postal application doesn't return. This seems especially likely for those applying from South American and Asian countries. It also seems to make a difference to which office you apply. The South African Swazi offices are always quick. If you have not heard within eight weeks, send a registered letter, stating your case, to: The Minister of Tourism, Commerce and Industry, P.O. Box 451, Mbabane, Swaziland. Tel. (09268) 43201, fax 2232.

These visa and permit hassles are not to dissuade visitors to Swaziland, but just the bureaucratic legacy left behind by the British administration, which the employment-orientated Swazis have happily continued.

For foreign visitors who are planning to travel on to Mozambique, visas can be obtained in Mbabane and take 12-48 hours.
Address: Embassy of the People's Republic of Mozambique, Vila Atinuke, Ezulwini, or P.O. Box 1212, Mbabane, Swaziland.
Tel. 43700.

If you get a temporary residence permit, allowing you to stay longer than 60 days, you will also need to get a tax clearance certificate before leaving the country. All this indicates is that you have not worked illegally in Swaziland, but rather have been self-supporting. Years ago, getting a tax clearance certificate was almost as traumatic as standing in line for a visa. Today it can be done in less than an hour. Go to the Treasury department's revenue office in Mbabane (tel. 42047), taking along your passport, visa, temporary residence permit and all your bank exchange receipts. Once you have the tax clearance certificate, put it away safely and forget about it, it's never asked for anyway.

CUSTOMS

The usual one litre of spirits and 400 cigarettes duty-free regulations apply in Swaziland. In addition to this allowance, 50 cigars, two litres of wine and 500 ml of perfume are permitted. Take note however, that visitors from the Common Customs Area are exempt from any duties and may bring in whatever quantities of these goods they like. There is one catch though; whatever you bring in has to be for personal use only.

On arrival at the border you will be required to fill in an entry/departure card. This form requests details of: title, surname, first names, place and date of birth, nationality, passport number, date of expiry, occupation, reason for entry/departure, duration, residential address in Swaziland, number of children accompanying, mode of travel, destination, car registration and passengers.

Take along a pen to fill in these forms, a sense of humour and saintly patience. Expect long queues, notably on Friday evenings and Sunday afternoons.

Tourists are supposed to fill in a baggage declaration form. If you bypass this regulation and get caught, not only are the goods likely to be permanently confiscated but you also risk the chance of a hefty fine, immediate deportation or a few hours in one of those notorious Swazi prisons. Visitors are unlikely to be bothered by customs control in Swaziland. Inspections are cursory, a few innocuous questions relating to firearms are occasionally asked and that is all. It should be over within five minutes, and then you are into Swaziland. Hitchhikers and backpackers though are frequently singled out for thorough searches. There is not a great deal one can do but comply. Be polite, smile a lot, and they soon lose interest.

The same regulations apply when returning to South Africa. While Swazi customs are mildly annoying, the South Africans are exasperating. Expect a thorough search no matter who you are or what your mode of travel. Cannabis, mandrax and gun trafficking are big business from Swaziland to South Africa. If you look like the archetypal backpacker: casual clothes, backpack, faraway look in the eyes and peaceful attitude, you are guaranteed an investigation that stops just short of a full body search.

Firearms are taboo in Swaziland. There are many weapons in Swaziland (travellers may notice that most of the remote village headmen are armed), but a tourist arriving with a gun will not receive a welcome.

If for some reason you feel that you need to be armed in Swaziland, apply at least six months in advance to: The Firearms Licensing Committee, P.O. Box 49, Mbabane, Swaziland. If no reply has been received in that time, you can safely assume that the application has been rejected. Further letters of inquiry will be met with the same silence.

There are no reasons why a visitor should even want to bring a great deal of goods into Swaziland. Prices are similar to those in South Africa. Standards of food and drink are excellent and shops are well stocked with all the necessities. With the country being so small, travellers can be back in the First-World cities of South Africa within a few hours. What is suggested, especially for those visitors who are travelling one of the described routes, is a Thermos flask that keeps liquids cold. For safari and macho types, a canvas water bag to hang out of your window while you drive around is also good.

For items not mentioned above, it is advisable to contact the relevant ministerial departments:
Department of Customs and Excise. Tel. (09268) 45370.
For pets, plants and other agricultural goods:
Ministry of Agriculture. Tel. (09268) 42731.

Opening and closing times for the main border posts are divided into different timetables. The times indicated below are merely guidelines as many of the smaller border posts work to a variable schedule.
Bulembu: 8h00-16h00 Gege: 8h00-16h00 Lavumisa: 7h00-20h00 Lomahasha: 7h00-20h00 Mahamba: 7h00-22h00 Mananga: 8h00-18h00 Matsamo: 8h00-18h00. Matsapha Airport: 7h00-22h00 Ngwenya: 7h00-22h00 Salitje: 8h00-16h00 Sandlane: 8h00-16h00 Sicunusa: 8h00-14h00.

MONEY

The Emalangeni (E) is divided into 100 cents. There are coins of two, five, 10, 20, 50 cents and one Lilangeni and notes of two, five, 10, 20, and 50 Emalangeni. Whatever you may hear to the contrary, South African rands are gladly accepted throughout Swaziland. In some places, fees are actually asked for in rands.

There is no limit to the amount of money you may bring into the country. Bear in mind though that Swazi money is not accepted in South Africa or any of the other countries in southern Africa. Should you change money in Swaziland, make certain that you are given a receipt for the transaction. Not many visitors ask for these but they are worth getting for two reasons. Firstly, you will need it when exchanging money when you depart Swaziland. Secondly, certain official documents require proof of financial transactions. This is particularly true if you intend staying in Swaziland longer than 60 days. They prove that you have been changing money while visiting the country and not earning income illegally.

In the larger urban centres, you can change foreign currency or cash travellers cheques at any of the international banking houses. The most common travellers cheques seen in Swaziland are Thomas Cook. Travellers often make the mistake of bringing too many small denomination cheques. Depending on your length of stay, it is better to only take along a few small denomination cheques, which you can use at the end of your visit. While in Swaziland, cash as much money as you feel safe carrying. Take advantage of the opportunity to change money. Banking in Swaziland is a nightmare for the foreign visitor. No-one really seems to know what's going on with the latest exchange rates and you will spend hours waiting for assistance. In the smaller towns, it is virtually impossible to change foreign currency or travellers cheques. Some of the large hotels also offer exchange services, but obviously at lower rates than banks. When getting cash in Swaziland remember two things: firstly, keep the spread of notes large. Trying to break down E50 can be difficult, especially away from towns. There seems to be a drastic shortage of change in Swaziland, and few visitors can afford to keep leaving the small change behind. Secondly, under no circumstances accept torn or damaged notes. Nobody will take them as payment, and even beggars can get vocally unhappy about being given torn money.

A word of caution: do not run out of money in Swaziland. Nothing can be done without money in the towns and cities. Travellers who have had this misfortune recommend putting a call through to someone at home for a money transfer and then heading out into the rural areas where money is not as important. Forget about trying to get money by mail. Bank transfers can also be very difficult. Not only will this take a long time, but the handling charges will be exorbitant. If you have no alternative, make sure that the money is sent to one of the large banks in Mbabane. Suggested institutions are:

Standard Chartered Bank, Allister Miller Street, Mbabane, Swaziland. Tel. 43351, fax 44060.

Meridien Bank, The Mall, Mbabane, Swaziland. Tel. 46208, fax 43088.

In Mbabane, Manzini, Siteki and Nhlangano there is a thriving black market in foreign currency. It is particularly strong in Mbabane. It is, of course, illegal.

Credit cards are accepted in all urban centres and at most tourist-class hotels and restaurants. At international banks in Mbabane, Manzini and Nhlangano credit cards can be used to draw cash. Handling charges are high for these transactions and visitors are advised to only use this as a last resort. Even though accepted in cities and large towns, once into the rural districts a credit card becomes useless.

Finally, arrive in Swaziland with sufficient funds, preferably in cash, to last your visit. To avoid the hassles of Emalangeni transactions, some visitors cross into one of the South African towns which are within a few kilometres of the main border posts, and draw rands there.

COSTS

It is difficult to estimate what a visit to Swaziland will cost. Major considerations are: mode of travel, standard of accommodation chosen and meals eaten. Getting around Swaziland is relatively inexpensive, while lazing around the pool at an hotel is expensive. If you decide to travel by public transport, staying in villages and camping, the trip will be cheap. By comparison, people who stay at hotels, see the country with an organised tour or spend evenings in the casino, will return home without much money.

Swaziland has a wide range of accommodation to suit all budgets. The secret of cheap lodgings is in getting to meet the locals. Those who are determined to be tourists will have to accept paying higher prices.

Most visitors will aim for something in between these extremes. Stay in reasonable hotels or inns, have two meals per day with a lunch-time snack, occasionally have late night entertainment, buy gifts and curios and visit a few of the game parks.

Keep in mind that this is Africa and what you pay does not always have a direct influence on the standard of service you can expect. Should you opt for a shoestring budget, it does good to sometimes splash out on a lavish meal at a fine restaurant, or a night at one of Swaziland's nightclubs. Not only is this good for relaxation, it also does wonders for your travel saturated mind.

DOCUMENTS

A passport is the most important document visitors will need. It is advisable to keep your passport with you at all times; even when in the casino or visiting a game reserve. Make certain that the expiry date allows for your entire stay in Swaziland and that, where necessary, there is a valid stamped visa.

An international health certificate will be required for foreigners entering from beyond the Common Customs Area. Few visitors arriving from Europe or the Americas are questioned about this document. But those arriving from other countries in Africa or Asia may be requested to present the signed and stamped booklet. These certificates can be obtained, prior to departure, from the Government Health Ministry in your country of residence.

Student cards and international youth hostel cards are useless in Swaziland. Few concessions are granted, mainly due to the influx of fake cards during the early eighties. Some small hotels give discounts to bona fide students, but it is negligible and not worth the effort. There have been reports of travellers using public transport being given lower fares on Zeeman's Passenger Service, P.O. Box 208, Mbabane, Swaziland. Tel. (09268) 61166. We were given an excellent discount by speaking to the driver of a Muhle-One-Way-Services bus. Address: P.O. Box 309, Mbabane, Swaziland. Tel. (09268) 43124.

Most visitors to Swaziland do so with their own transport. If arriving from countries within the Common Customs Area no special license or permit is required. However, drivers from outside these areas or those intending to hire a vehicle in Swaziland, will need to be in possession of an international driving permit. These can be arranged through motoring organisations in your home country. The most efficient and helpful are the branch offices of the Automobile Association (AA). They issue the permit within 14 days – provided of course you are over 18 and already have a valid license.

In addition to the above documents, it is always a good idea to take along at least four passport-sized black and white photographs. These will be necessary if you intend applying for a visa or an extension. Take photocopies of all these documents, plus the first three pages of your passport. Put these in a safe place until needed. Journalists and photographers are not allowed to work without first getting a press accreditation card from the Ministry of Information. Apply at least two months in advance.

Address: Ministry of Information, P.O. Box 388, Mbabane, Swaziland.
Telephone: (09268) 42761, fax 42774.

TIPPING

As in most African countries, tipping in Swaziland is unheard of. Visitors will find, however, that a tip to the right person goes a long way in smoothing your stay in Swaziland. These tips should not be given in the manner of "western" tips. In Swaziland, tipping is more for getting something done. A suitable tip to the visa clerk will get you a stamped extension within four hours.

Tipping in Swaziland will provide a whole range of pleasant surprises. Bus drivers and guides are not usually tipped. If staying at an hotel for more than a day, tipping will get you excellent service and personal attention each time you appear. Be judicious in your tipping, or you may find yourself running out of money within a few days.

In tourist-class restaurants the 10 per cent tax added to the bill is enough to deter most foreigners from adding their customary tip to the bill. Leave something, though, as the low wages and large families in Swaziland mean that each extra cent is desperately needed.

CONSULATES AND EMBASSIES

Most countries that have consular representatives in Swaziland have their main offices in the capital, Mbabane. Few countries, however, do have consulates or embassies in Swaziland. If desperate, get yourself to South Africa and the numerous diplomatic missions found in Pretoria. Those countries that have offices in Swaziland are:

The Royal Belgian Consulate
Address: (Postal) P.O. Box 124, Malkerns, Swaziland.
             (Physical) Office No. 3, 2nd Floor, Independence House,
             Johnson St, Mbabane.
Telephone: (09268) 83180.

British High Commission
Address: (Postal) Private Bag Mbabane, Mbabane, Swaziland.
             (Physical) British High Commission Building, Allister Miller
             St, Mbabane.
Telephone: (09268) 42581, fax 42585.

Embassy of the Republic of China

Address: (Postal) P.O. Box 56, Mbabane, Swaziland.
(Physical) Warner St, Mbabane.
Telephone: (09268) 42379, fax 42109.

The Royal Danish Consulate

Address: (Postal) P.O. Box 815, Mbabane, Swaziland.
(Physical) Sokhamlilo Building, Johnson St, Mbabane.
Telephone: (09268) 43547, fax 43548.

European Communities Commission

Address: (Postal) P.O. Box A36, Swazi Plaza, Mbabane, Swaziland.
(Physical) Dhlan'ubeka House, corner Tin and Walker St,
Mbabane.
Telephone: (09268) 42908, fax 46729.

Embassy of the Republic of Germany

Address: (Postal) P.O. Box 1507, Mbabane, Swaziland.
(Physical) Dhlan'ubeka House, corner Tin and Walker St,
Mbabane.
Telephone: (09268) 43174.

The Israeli Embassy

Address: (Postal) P.O. Box 146, Mbabane, Swaziland.
(Physical) Mbabane House, Warner St, Mbabane.
Telephone: (09268) 42626, fax 45857.

The Italian Consulate

Address: (Postal) P.O. Box 928, Manzini, Swaziland.
(Physical) 219 Tenbergen St, Manzini.
Telephone: (09268) 52436, fax 52436.

Embassy of the Republic of Korea

Address: (Postal) P.O. Box 2074, Mbabane, Swaziland.
(Physical) Dhlan'ubeka House, corner Tin and Walker St,
Mbabane.
Telephone: (09268) 45568.

Embassy of the People's Republic of Mozambique
Address: (Postal) P.O. Box 1212, Mbabane, Swaziland.
            (Physical) Princess Dr., Mbabane.
Telephone: (09268) 43700, telex 2248WD.

Consulate of the Netherlands
Address: (Postal) P.O. Box 1205, Mbabane, Swaziland.
            (Physical) Business Machines House, Sheffield Rd, Industrial Site, Mbabane.
Telephone: (09268) 45178, fax 44006.

Consulate of Portugal
Address: (Postal) P.O. Box 855, Mbabane, Swaziland.
Telephone: (09268) 46780, fax 46770.

The South African Trade Mission
Address: (Postal) P.O. Box 2597, Mbabane, Swaziland.
            (Physical) Allister Miller St, Mbabane.
Telephone: (09268) 44651, fax 46944.

Embassy of the United States of America
Address: (Postal) P.O. Box 199, Mbabane, Swaziland.
            (Physical) Central Bank Building, Warner St, Mbabane.
Telephone: (09268) 22018/44952, fax 46446

SWAZILAND DIPLOMATIC MISSIONS ABROAD

Belgium
Embassy of the Kingdom of Swaziland
Address: Rue Joseph 11-71, 1040 Brussels, Belgium.
Telephone: 02-230-01-069.

Canada
Swaziland High Commission
Address: 130 Albert St, Ottawa, Ontario KIP PG4, Canada.
Telephone: 5671480.

Denmark

Embassy of the Kingdom of Swaziland
Address: Kastelsvej 19, DK-2100 Copenhagen, Denmark.
Telephone: 426111.

Germany

Consulate of the Kingdom of Swaziland
Address: 4-D Dusseldorf 1, Worringer Strasse 59, Germany.

Greece

Consulate of the Kingdom of Swaziland
Address: 88 Drossopoulou, Athens 804, Greece.

Japan

Consulate of the Kingdom of Swaziland
Address: 1 Kanda Uzumi-cho, Chiyoda-ku, Tokyo 101, Japan.

Kenya

High Commission of the Kingdom of Swaziland
Address: P.O. Box 41887, Nairobi, Kenya.

Republic of Korea

Embassy of the Kingdom of Swaziland
Address: K.P.O. Box 1427, Seoul, Republic of Korea.
Telephone: 7440263.

Mozambique

Embassy of the Kingdom of Swaziland
Address: P.O. Box 4711, Maputo, Mozambique.
Telephone: 492451.

Spain

Consulate of the Kingdom of Swaziland
Address: R. Casa Ortego, Madrid, Spain.

South Africa

Swaziland Trade Mission
Address: P.O. Box 8030, Johannesburg 2000, South Africa.
Telephone: 299776.

Taiwan

Consulate of the Kingdom of Swaziland
Address: 53 Nanking, East Rd., Section 2, Taipei, Taiwan.

United Kingdom

High Commission of the Kingdom of Swaziland
Address: 58 Pont St, Knightsbridge, London SW1, England.
Telephone: 5814976.

United States of America

Embassy of the Kingdom of Swaziland
Address: Suite 141, Van Ness Centre, 4301 Connecticut Ave., Wash-
             ington DC, United States of America.
Telephone: 202-362-6683.

TOURIST INFORMATION

Tourist offices

The Swaziland Government Tourist Office has limited representation
outside the country. In Swaziland, visitors can obtain several leaflets,
maps and booklets. These booklets are particularly good as they offer
suggested itineraries for Mbabane and the rest of the country. Prior to
starting a journey through Swaziland it is advisable to visit the Tourist
Office in the Swazi Plaza, Mbabane, or write for information: Swaziland
Government Tourist Office, P.O. Box 451, Mbabane, Swaziland. Tel.
(09268) 43201. Visitors from overseas could try getting tourist information from the nearest diplomatic representative of Swaziland. There
is a problem with these contacts though. Often the information they
supply is hopelessly outdated. It is better to contact the tourism offices
in Swaziland. Make enquiries at least three months ahead of departure.

   Many hotels and inns are also able to provide useful information to
visitors. Ask for tourist information if you make prior hotel or inn
bookings. The Pigg's Peak Hotel and Casino is particularly good at
providing loads of pamphlets and reading material.

Postal services

Swaziland's postal service is archaic and slow. Poste restante is unheard
of outside the major urban centres of Mbabane and Manzini. If post is
sent outside of these cities, rather have it addressed to the hotel or inn

where you are staying. Even then, you can expect anything from three weeks to three months for a letter to arrive from Europe, and even longer from the Americas. People who send you mail should address it as follows: Surname in capitals and underlined, then your first names, the poste restante post office, town and finally, Swaziland. Finding mail can be difficult, so check under both your surname and first names. One French visitor found her letter filed under the name of the sender!

When sending post, expect a long wait. Be patient and take a book to read. If needed, buy stamps from one of the international hotel reception desks.

Telephone

Swaziland's telephone system is efficient but expensive. Calls beyond southern Africa from rural post offices need to be pre-booked. In the larger towns you can expect almost instant link-up. While in cities connections are good, country lines are frequently so full of static and eavesdroppers that you will hardly be able to hear the other person. You can also phone direct to most points in southern Africa from Matsapha Airport. Have a lot of change ready if using a public phone; they eat coins at an amazing rate. Telephone calls around Swaziland are instantaneous with remarkably clear lines.

Telex

International telex services from Swaziland are excellent, seldom used and surprisingly cheap in comparison to telephones and faxes. Although the fax is rapidly ousting the telex, many embassies, hotels, international businesses, government ministries and missions still operate a telex. Most post offices have a telex that is available for public use, as are the telex facilities at top-class hotels.

Time

Greenwich Mean Time plus two hours throughout the year.

Business hours

Shops – Monday to Friday: 8h00-17h00
         Saturday: 8h30-13h00.
Offices – Monday to Friday: 8h00-13h00 and 14h00-17h00
          Saturday: 8h00-13h00. (This excludes all government offices which are closed on Saturday.)

Banks – Monday to Friday: 8h30-14h30
          Saturday: 8h30-11h00.
Post office – Monday to Friday: 8h00-13h00 and 14h00-17h00
          Saturday: 8h00-11h00.
On Sundays, all offices and banks and most shops are closed. However, hotel banking services usually operate from about 8h00-22h00. Eating establishments fall into three categories: snack bars which are open from around 7h30-16h00; restaurants normally open from 10h30-23h00; eating houses open from 8h00-0h00. Street vendors can be found selling between 7h00-18h00.

MEDIA

There are several newspapers available in Swaziland. Two English language newspapers are on sale daily in the main centres. They are the *Swazi Observer* and *The Times of Swaziland. The Weekend Observer* is on sale on Saturday, with the *Sunday Times* being available, obviously, on Sunday. In SiSwati, *Tikhatsi Temaswati* is published daily. South African dailies are also available as are South African Sunday papers. All these newspapers cover current world events, with the Swazi papers including detailed local events.

No glossy Swazi magazines are published, but a large number of South African and international periodicals are on sale at bookstores and top-class hotels.

Swaziland has a number of radio stations and a local television network. The South African Broadcasting Corporation's channels can also be picked up. Swazi television is not very good, and you will end up in at least one conversation about the poor quality of local television. Outside towns, visitors are unlikely to find a television set. Instead, radios are the communication link with the rest of the country and occasionally the world. Few visitors have time to sit watching television or listening to the radio. Most newsworthy information will be found by glancing at newspapers.

SPORTS

Soccer is avidly followed by the Swazis. From the stadiums of urban settlements to sand pitches in the most isolated areas, visitors will find people playing soccer. Over weekends, matches take place throughout the country. Visitors should make an effort to see at least one game.

When international matches against the Swazi national team are played, you will find groups of men and youths huddled around radios listening to the latest score and commentary.

Golf is the favourite tourist game. Most of the tourist-class hotels have their own courses. A few have nine-hole courses, while almost all company-owned towns have country clubs that offer visitors temporary membership. Top of the range is undoubtedly the world renowned 18-hole golf course at the Royal Swazi Sun. Prior arrangements to play can be made by contacting: The Activities Manager, Royal Swazi Sun Hotel and Casino, P.O. Box 412, Mbabane, Swaziland. Tel. (09268) 61001, fax 61606.

HEALTH

Apart from visitors who are residents of countries in the Common Customs Area, all other people entering Swaziland require an international immunisation certificate. Yellow fever, cholera and polio immunisations must be valid. Not required but highly recommended is an injection against infectious hepatitis A, plus another for tetanus. A course of tablets against typhoid should also be taken.

A good book to take along is the Ross Institute of Tropical Hygiene's, *Preservation of Personal Health in Warm Climates.* The book can be ordered directly from the institute at: Ross Institute, Keppel St, London, WC1, England. Take along your own first-aid kit, remembering to include sealed hypodermics. AIDS has become a serious problem in Swaziland. Although few cases are ever acknowledged publicly, in most settlements the people are aware of AIDS. Be especially careful if you expect to have sexual intercourse. Condoms are the safest choice, but in the larger centres where prostitution is rampant, abstinence is the best form of protection.

Of importance to travellers in Swaziland is the high incidence of bilharzia and malaria. While tourists will be returning home to good medical facilities, travellers may have to spend several days or weeks on the road. Although not necessary for the short-term visitor, some form of medical insurance is vital for those who intend staying longer than 30 days in Swaziland. There are a number of policies on the market. Contact any travel agent for further details. The Travel Assistance Company is recommended; ask about the Leisure Travel options.
Address: P.O. Box 4352, Johannesburg, 2000, South Africa.
Telephone: (011) 838-6311, fax 834-2633.

Bilharzia

Infection of the bladder and large intestine by blood flukes (worms) causes a painful debilitating illness. It is self-propagating if not treated. If in doubt, contact the nearest clinic, hospital or medical service. The Tourist office claims that the highland rivers and dams are free of bilharzia, but to be safe, avoid swimming in any river, stream or dam in Swaziland.

Malaria

Endemic to most of the country, the areas in the south and east have especially bad reputations for malaria. The female anopheles mosquito blood-parasite spreads the disease. Anopheles usually fly in the hours of darkness. A single bite from an infected mosquito is enough to cause the disease. Numerous drugs have been used over the years to combat this illness, but the mosquitoes just as quickly develop immunity. Check with your doctor for the latest recommendation. At the time of going to press, the recommended anti-malaria programme consisted of the following: chloroquine (trade names: Nivaquine tablets and syrup, or Plasmoquine capsules) 400 mg (adults) once per week, on the same day each week, plus proguanil (trade name: Paludrine tablets) 200 mg (adults) daily. Another frequently used prophylaxis, mefloquine (trade name: Lariam tablets) should only be followed with medical prescription and monitoring. Commence within a few days prior to entering Swaziland, and continue for at least four weeks after leaving the country. Anti-malaria programmes are costly, but this is something visitors should not skimp on.

Symptoms of malaria are shivering, high fever and severe headaches. The diagnosis should be verified as soon as possible. Medical advice can be sought at virtually all lowland clinics and hospitals. The missions too, always have someone familiar with treatment. If you are isolated and unable to reach a medical unit, the recommended emergency treatment consists of: 600 mg (four tablets) of chloroquine all at once, followed by 300 mg (two tablets) six hours later, with two tablets on each successive day. In chloroquine-resistant regions take one dose of three Fansidar tablets. Take along insect repellent or mosquito coils for the evenings. If possible include a mosquito net in your luggage. These can be bought from most outdoor shops and fit snugly into a small space.

Diarrhoea

Spend enough time in Swaziland, especially in the rural areas, and you are likely to have at least one bout of diarrhoea. Often it is the change of diet or water that causes the illness. Do not immediately dose yourself with Lomotil. At first, revert to a liquid diet for a few days. Your body dehydrates quickly with diarrhoea, so fluids must be taken in larger amounts than normal. Stay off dairy products as well. If this does not help after a few days, contact a clinic or doctor who will prescribe suitable medication. Should you be planning on hiking, take along a packet of Lomotil tablets for severe diarrhoea.

Health in Swaziland rarely presents problems to those who have taken precautions. The climate is healthy, warm and enjoyable. Most visitors return home suntanned and relaxed.

CLOTHING

If you are planning to spend most of your visit in the smart hotels of the Ezulwini valley, Mbabane or Manzini, you will need to take along a good selection of clothing. Hotels in these areas have high standards as regards dress, particularly in the evenings. Visitors to top-class hotels and casinos should take along a jacket, dress shirt and smart trousers. Women should include an evening dress. Casual wear during the day is accepted within limits. Shorts, polo shirts, blouses and shoes are the norm.

On the other hand, if you will be spending most of your time in the more casual, remoter regions of the country, take along as little as possible. Throughout the country shirtsleeves and shorts will be adequate during the day. At night, in the highlands, you may need a light jersey. In winter, take along a jacket if visiting the western highland forest districts.

Going without a shirt is not regarded as suitable dress for male visitors. A suggested list of clothing for a visit to Swaziland would look something like this:

Jeans, shorts, underwear, running shoes, hiking boots, plastic sandals, swimming costume, short-sleeved shirts, T-shirts, raincoat, light jersey, windbreaker and a set of smart clothes.

In addition to the abovementioned clothing, remember to include: toiletries, first-aid kit, small combination locks, hat, sunglasses and a sewing kit. If exploring Swaziland during the wet summer months, include a plastic poncho, gaiters for hiking and possibly even an umbrella (which can be sold or traded when it comes time to leave).

A combination lock is necessary for visitors staying in sleazier accommodation in large urban centres. This can be put onto the door if you need to leave your luggage in the room. The same lock can be used to padlock your pack to a bus seat on long journeys, when you are likely to fall asleep. Another useful item is a sink plug. Make certain to get a universal size. Cheap accommodation seldom has bath or basin plugs, and it can be frustrating trying to wash when the water keeps disappearing. A pen-knife will come to your rescue countless times while travelling in Swaziland. From peeling fruit to slicing bread, from opening cartons to holding food, a knife is a necessity for budget travellers. If travelling by car, consider an electric hot-water element that can be plugged into the cigarette lighter point.

A clothesline and pegs should be added if you are going to do a lot of wilderness camping. Torches with spare batteries are also important if venturing to outlying districts. Insect repellent or smouldering coils are recommended throughout the year. People who wear glasses should bring along a prescription for a replacement pair. Should your glasses break they can be fixed or replaced within a few hours in Mbabane or Manzini. Contact Oskar Walch, Swazi Plaza, Mbabane. Tel. 42816, or Mabele Heights Building, Manzini. Tel. 52665. Vision Care Centre, The Mall, Mbabane. Tel. 46933. Emergency number 44845.

Visiting Swaziland in summer demands attention to sunburn. The sun is fierce, especially in the eastern lowlands. Apply suntan cream whenever you go out during the day. Hiking in hot weather requires forethought. A hat, sun cream (minimum factor eight), glasses and water bottle all contribute to making a trip enjoyable. Dehydration sets in quickly as the body sweats in the humidity and heat. Either carry fortified energy drinks, pure water or stop frequently for cups of tea. If hiking for longer than four hours, consider wearing a long-sleeved shirt to prevent your arms getting severely burned.

Toiletries are not a problem as most can be bought at reasonable prices in all towns and most villages. A shaving kit will be useful if staying in one of the smarter hotels. Instead of the hassle of daily shaving, every second or third day nip down to the local barber. These men can be found in every settlement. They will willingly shave you in their shopfronts, while a crowd of children inevitably gathers to watch.

There is really no need to cart along a sleeping bag if staying at hotels and inns. On the other hand, if tribal villages are your destination, a sleeping bag or light sheet is worthwhile. Visitors on shoestring budgets are advised to also carry a plastic sheet that can be used to cover dubious beds. Unlike in many African countries, you do not have to carry your own toilet paper. This is obtainable at even the remotest store.

WOMEN VISITORS

Swaziland will present problems to solo women travellers, but do not be put off by this. With a little care, planning and common sense, there is no reason why a woman should not have an enjoyable trip around the country.

Before getting on to safety, a mention concerning women's health needs to be made. With a change of diet to a mainly starch and high protein intake, many women may find themselves with a lowered resistance to infection. This, coupled with the heat and humidity of Swaziland, may lead to certain vaginal infections. Wear cotton underwear, loose-fitting skirts and keep the vaginal area clean. Yeast infections are not uncommon among women visitors. Characterised by itching, a rash and occasionally a discharge, the infection can be treated with a douche of lemon juice or vinegar. If you are worried about this, include Nystatin suppositories in your first-aid kit. A burning sensation on urination, with pain and a discharge, could be due to a *Trichomonas* infection. A prescription of flagyl drugs is suggested, which will have to be obtained from a doctor. Tampons can be found in most urban centres. They are reasonably priced and come in a variety of choices.

Safety should be the most important criteria for women travellers. The Ezulwini valley has the worst reputation. Do not wander around alone in this region, including the Mlilwane Game Sanctuary. Try and get a companion to travel with. Even on buses and in taxis, you are likely to be bothered by men. At hotels and inns, drunks will try to make themselves comfortable at your table, even though uninvited. Many hotel managers and security staff seem either reluctant or unable to help. Avoid getting involved in sexual conversations; the male Swazi view of females is not very high – cattle have more worth.

Attention to mode of dress will go a long way in easing the journey. Under no circumstances attempt to imitate Swazi women by walking about without a top on. Not only can you be certain of being molested, but are guaranteed to be arrested. Also, do not wear very short skirts or shorts.

Stay away from squatter settlements and obviously poorer areas of towns. At night, keep to well-lit hotels and inns, and never go walking through the streets of a city alone after sunset. In the remote districts, women are quite safe. The strong family structure and importance of the mother, results in a safe stay for most women visitors. Try to sleep in settlements rather than open bush. You will be welcomed and treated with respect.

Expect to be bothered at some stage of your journey. Keep calm or get up and leave. By following simple safety guidelines women travellers may well have as pleasant a trip as any male visitor.

PHOTOGRAPHY

Plagued by cross-border raids, wedged in between a country until recently at war, Mozambique, on the one side, and arguably the most militarily powerful country on the African continent, South Africa, on three sides, Swaziland's officials are suspicious of cameras and photographers. In cities, journalists and the press are regarded as little more than vultures and even getting a press accreditation card is something of a trial. Politics aside, in the remote valleys and mountains the dislike of photography has to do with tribal beliefs.

Never take photographs of anything connected with the military or police. In addition, do not take pictures of bridges, communication stations or prisons. Border posts are also taboo. To be on the safe side, always ask permission before clicking away. This applies both to people and installations. Show respect for people's wishes. On the tourist trail, expect to have to pay to take photographs of villages or Swazis. In the kraals, check with the headman before taking photos.

It is not necessary to take along all your own film requirements. Fotorama at the Swazi Plaza in Mbabane sell and develop film.

Batteries can be found in all urban centres, but it might be a good idea to take along your own if planning to head out into the wilderness areas.

Should you be forced to buy film at one of the small photo-studios dotted around Swaziland, check the expiry date of the film. You may find it difficult getting anything over 100 ASA at these places. The ideal for this sort of travel photography is 64 ASA.

Place all exposed film into lead-lined packets for safekeeping. If staying at hotels, photographers should carry their spare film in coolbags, getting the packs re-chilled in fridges overnight. Some form of travel insurance is highly recommended, remembering to specify items over a certain value. Swaziland will provide countless opportunities for photographers.

SECURITY

Theft is a worsening problem in Swaziland. Around the tourist areas, such as between Mbabane and Manzini, robbery has reached epidemic proportions. Any loss involving documents entails hours of filling in statements with the Royal Swazi Police and the chances that the items will be recovered are slight. However, with caution and planning, one can avoid having anything stolen.

Make certain to lock your room when leaving. At hotels do not hand keys in, but carry them with you. (If lost, hotels have master keys anyway.) Even at night, when sleeping, it is advisable that your door be locked. Never leave any valuable travel documents, large quantities of cash or travellers cheques in your room. While all hotels have security facilities, visitors should keep all documents on themselves. Splitting up cash and travellers cheques is recommended. Put some in a money-pouch, in your pockets and a little hidden somewhere in your luggage. Waist-pouches have proved a problem in Swaziland. Obviously holding money, these leather or canvas bags are easily cut or ripped. A solution is the money-pouch which hangs around the neck and down inside your shirt.

If taking a long bus ride, chain your luggage either to the roof or onto your seat. Because of the heat in the country, many people find themselves falling asleep on bus journeys.

Resist the temptation to stroll around with lots of camera gear slung over your shoulder. Be careful in large crowds. At bus depots, there are always many people moving about; should something be snatched it will disappear into the multitude within seconds. The worst reports have come from the bus depot in Mbabane. In Mbabane, youths work in teams; passing stolen items quickly from one to the other so you lose sight of them.

Other places with bad reputations are Nhlangano and Siteki.

Never leave your bags unattended on a bus. Get the assistant to strap them to the roof or carry them around until it is time to leave. Sadly, it is not only the locals you need to beware of. Other travellers can also present problems. Many of the travellers in the eastern and southern areas of Swaziland are travelling on a shoestring. Reports of stolen sleeping bags, books and camera equipment are not uncommon. This crime wave is not exclusive to the tourist areas though. The old Tea Road which goes from east of Mbabane, through the Mdzimba hills to exit near Manzini is notorious for attacks on visitors. But in the far northern districts, crime is rare. There, in the kraals and mud villages visitors can safely leave their belongings in one of the huts and go wandering with tribesmen.

Arrange a travel insurance policy before leaving. Travellers cheques should be replaceable if stolen. A full record of cheque numbers and all transactions should be kept. These records will need to be produced for a refund claim. No companies instantly replace amounts in excess of $US 1 000. To avoid any possible cash flow problems, keep a separate supply of emergency money, preferably in local currency.

As American Express has offices in both Mbabane and Manzini, this is a good reason to purchase their travellers cheques. Address: American Express (trading as Manica Travel Service), Development House, Swazi Plaza, Mbabane, tel. 42101 or 42298, and Manzini, at Manica House, Nkoseluhlaza Street, tel. 52237 or 52872. If cheques do get stolen, notify the police and an American Express office as soon as possible.

Beyond cities, large towns and heavily populated areas, it is unlikely that any crime will be committed against a foreign visitor. If accosted, under no circumstances retaliate. There is a steady flow of illegal weapons into Swaziland from Mozambique, and as a result many desperate people are armed. Give the assailants what they want and then report the matter. In remote areas, the best person to contact in the event of a crime is a village headman or district chief.

PLACES TO STAY

Accommodation for tourists used to luxury hotels is limited in Swaziland. Those prepared to experience a little discomfort in exchange for getting to know the Swazi, will never be without a place to stay.

High tariff

International class hotels occur only in three areas of the country. The most expensive and luxurious hotels are found down the Ezulwini valley. Alongside the main Mbabane-Manzini road, their ostentatious signs are a frequent sight. Well-known Sun International Resorts run a few high-priced, popular top-class hotels and casinos in the kingdom.

For sheer indulgence and pampering, nothing can beat a stay at the Royal Swazi Sun and Casino in the Ezulwini valley. Highly recommended is the quiet and splendid Mountain Inn, less than two km from Mbabane. In the north-west, the Pigg's Peak Protea Hotel and Casino has excellent service and genuine grandeur. In the far south of the country the Nhlangano Sun Hotel and Casino is pricey with poor service. One consideration at the expensive hotels is the infamous extras which are added to your bill. These include such absurdities as toiletries, morning tea or towel use at the pool. A 10 per cent tax is charged throughout the country.

Medium tariff

In almost every town of over 5 000 inhabitants you will find either an hotel or inn. These establishments offer basic but functional accommodation in reasonably-priced rooms. Meals are not always supplied, and guests should check this on registration. At most of the mid-range places there will be someone to cook you a meal if you provide the supplies. These inns and hotels are usually family-run, with homely atmospheres and interesting pubs. Rated as one of the best is the Highland Inn near Pigg's Peak. For visitors to the eastern parts of the country, little can compare with the Bend Inn in Big Bend. To the south, the Assegai Hotel in Hlatikulu is cheap and clean. In the north, Impala Arms makes a comfortable and attractive stop for visitors. Down the Ezulwini valley prices are high. A cheaper alternative is to stay in one of the beehive huts or cottages at enchanting Mlilwane Game Sanctuary.

Low tariff

It is possible to see the whole country at very low cost. Provided you are willing to sleep in huts or on the floor, or share with a family, you will have no problem in finding cheap accommodation. Part of the joy of travelling in Swaziland like this is the opportunity for living with and getting to know clans of the district. Should you consider this option, take along a sleeping bag. Washing facilities will, for the most part, be nonexistent. However, if you bring along your own soap and are willing to risk bilharzia, there are countless rivers and streams spread across the country.

Negotiate some recompense with the village headman or family patriarch. Food is always welcome. You will be taken in as part of the family and will eat with them. Provide variety to their meal by offering some of your tinned food, or cook them some dehydrated meals. Whenever you make use of this hospitality, bear in mind those visitors who will pass that way after you. If stuck for shelter, approach the nearest kraal or village and ask for the "Nkosi" or "Induna." Once admitted, request shelter for the night. No report has ever come out of Swaziland of a traveller being turned away from isolated villages and kraals.

FOOD

Food could be a big disappointment in Swaziland. Away from the tourist haunts, visitors are required to eat what the locals do; porridge, vegetables and meat. Vegetarians may have a hard time finding meals at the hotels and inns (Mountain Inn excluded; it has a specific vegetarian menu). Meat is not prepared in the Western way. In rural Swaziland, it is either roasted or broiled.

No food is taboo and visitors may be offered oddities such as cat or bull testicles. Traditional meals are filling, cheap and while bland, go a long way in keeping your expenses down. Fruit is always available at markets or villages.

Dairy products and meat in isolated settlements need to be treated with caution. Hygiene is not of a high standard by Western measures. Animals are slaughtered and then hung to bleed for a few hours. Flies soon descend in clouds, vomiting out a number of diseases into the carcass. Cows are not tested nor treated for tuberculosis or anthrax. Stay away from dairy products. Never buy eggs that have been standing on a shelf for a long time. In kraals, eggs are fresh and tasty but stores keep eggs for several weeks. Salmonella E. is rapidly becoming a problem in many countries, including neighbouring South Africa. It can cause death if the correct treatment is not immediately given.

Mozambique peri-peri chicken seems a ubiquitous dish in Swaziland. Hot, spicy and delicious, this meal is a speciality of the Woodcutter's Den near Pigg's Peak. Meat is available everywhere. From grilled steaks at international hotels, to stewed goat in the hill villages, visitors will find some form of meat eaten with virtually every meal. Roasted porridge is the staple of every traditional meal. There are numerous variations on how it is presented. At breakfast it is eaten with milk or as a gruel. Lunch will find it hard, broken into pieces and eaten with boiled chicken or mutton. Dinner sees the porridge pliable. A wad is taken from the pot and rolled into a ball which is then dipped in sauce and enjoyed with beef and a few greens.

For special dietary meals you should inform the hotel manager or receptionist on arrival. People hiking can provide for themselves by carrying some milled maize with them. Mixed with boiled water and cooked over a fire, you will soon be eating what the Swazis have had for decades.

Alcohol is cheap in Swaziland. Canned beer, bottled spirits and cocktails are available at all international hotels. Alcohol can also be bought from bottle stores, trading stores and illicit drinking houses in the shanty areas. Cereal beer is the traditional alcoholic beverage drunk by the Swazi. You will find this on sale at many villages across the country. The sign that traditional brew is on sale is a white rag or plastic packet tied to a tall pole. The brew's effect is slow but dramatic, so don't plan any driving, hiking or exploring afterwards.

Cold-drinks can be bought from all food shops, hotels, trading stores and bottle stores. Swaziland is hot, and many visitors find themselves drinking a lot more cold-drink than usual. Sweetened drinks do not quench the thirst for a long time. Rather drink clean water, tea or soda water. Water, other than from hotels, should not be drunk untreated. Iodine drops, purification tablets or water-purifying gadgets are advised for travellers who go into remote districts.

Away from hotels, the lack of variation in dishes can become depressing. Consider a few packets of dehydrated food, eating fresh fruit and a course of multivitamins. Do not make the mistake however, of not eating a few traditional Swazi meals.

Fast foods and takeaways are common in cities and urban centres. Selling hamburgers, chips, pies and sausages, they are a favourite with Swazi youth. In small towns, takeaways offer basic food such as porridge, sausage or beef, fish and chips and enormous fresh bread sandwiches with tomato, cheese and onion.

BOOKS AND MAPS

There are not many books devoted entirely to guiding a visitor through Swaziland. Those that cover the country do so either in the form of a tourist information book, or include Swaziland with other southern African countries. Some pre-trip reading is essential if you are to get the most out of a visit.

- *South Africa, Lesotho, Swaziland,* Lonely Planet Guide Books (Lonely Planet Publications, Victoria, Australia)

  A short, detailed chapter on Swaziland makes this a useful book for travellers who are visiting the entire region. Aimed at the budget traveller, this book includes valuable information on cheap accommodation, transport and hints for backpackers. If you are planning to go on to South Africa or Lesotho, this book will prove a valuable addition to your mobile library.

- *Swaziland Jumbo Tourist Guide,* Hazel Hussey (R.O. Hussey & Company, Mbabane, Swaziland)

  Claimed by its publishers to be internationally recognised as the official Swaziland tourist guide, this book has the dubious format of being full of advertising. It does, however, offer useful and interesting information on Swazi history, tourist requirements, services and facilities. Updated regularly, it tends to be biased in favour of advertisers, often not detailing accommodation if no sponsorship has been forthcoming. This guide will prove helpful to visitors who have money to spend. Details on tourist handicraft shops, medium to top class hotels and lists of useful addresses are included.

- *Abantu,* Martin West and Jean Morris (Struik Publishers, Cape Town, South Africa)

  Visitors interested in cultural history and tradition would do well to read this book. There is a section on the Swazi people's history, beliefs, rituals, traditions and politics. This book is excellent pre-trip reading and it will make the problems that are bound to crop up in Swaziland that much more understandable.

- *The Mlilwane Story,* Terence E. Reilly (Terence and Liz Reilly, Mlilwane Trust, Swaziland)

  This book relates the development of conservation in Swaziland. Written by Swaziland's most famous wildlife figure, it is packed with history, anecdotes, information and details on the game reserves under the auspices of Big Game Parks of Swaziland Holdings. This book is definitely worth buying on arrival in Swaziland.

Choosing a map with which to travel through Swaziland is dependent on the sort of touring you plan. The Automobile Association's *Motoring in Swaziland* is probably the best general purpose map available. With a scale of 1:535 000, it includes enough detail to make a journey with your own transport. A key identifies hotels, fuel, airports, forests and places of interest. There are mistakes concerning distances and roads. Small inset maps of Mbabane and Manzini give the city roads and show points of interest to visitors. This map can be obtained from the Automobile Association of South Africa, P.O. Box 596, Johannesburg, South Africa.

A tourist map is available from the Swaziland Tourist Office in Mbabane. This map can also be ordered directly from the Ministry of Commerce, Industry and Tourism, P.O. Box 451, Mbabane, Swaziland. Tel. (09268) 43201/6. It shows the main through-routes, and an overleaf section provides general tourist information.

A more detailed map showing roads, rivers, mountains and hills, as well as game reserves, is available from Map Studio in South Africa. Address: Map Studio, P.O. Box 624, Bergvlei, 2012, South Africa. Tel. (011) 4449473, fax 4449472. Much smaller than the AA map, the scale is 1:800 000. It has the advantage of including far more rivers and points of interest to visitors.

Hikers and walkers should purchase a topographical map from the Department of Geological Survey and Mines, cnr. Johnston and Walker Streets, Mbabane, Swaziland. Tel. (09268) 42411/45215. Get this map prior to leaving for Swaziland as it will be useful in planning hiking routes. Some knowledge of map and compass reading will be an advantage if you are venturing into the wilderness regions. Very necessary on the trail, this map can be cumbersome due to its size. A solution is to photocopy only that section which you need for the trip.

At the start of each chapter which covers a region, the *Swaziland Jumbo Tourist Guide* has a small map showing the particular area covered. These insert maps do not show smaller settlements but concentrate on towns that will be seen on the tourist trail.

The recommended maps are: If travelling with your own transport: the AA road map. Hiking or exploring the remote regions: a Swaziland topographical map. For general pre-trip information and planning, use the map from Map Studio.

THINGS TO BUY

World famous for its handicrafts, Swaziland is full of wonderful things to purchase. Visitors will find numerous shops and village industries producing intricate and beautiful handwork. In rural areas you will discover arts and crafts made with techniques that are as old as Swazi history. In curio shops, prices are fixed and usually high. In remote settlements, travellers will find products just as good as those in towns, without a set price. Remember to bargain when buying at these tribal villages. Do not be hesitant in setting a figure. Mirth and debates can be expected. Finally a fee will be reached that is amenable to both. When you compare these prices with those in shops you will have a better idea of the item's worth.

Obtain some knowledge of the Swazi handicraft trade by doing a little research before leaving on your trip.

Typical of traditional societies, most artists are male. However, while their major source of income is from the sale of handicrafts, subsistence farming remains important. Because of these dual occupations, the quantity of crafts available is limited. Despite this, the handicrafts on sale are a delight and source of great interest. Each item is made with care and commitment – the Swazi believe that a part of the artist exists in everything they create.

In cities, visitors will see how the enterprising Swazis have adapted their designs to modern materials. T-shirts with elaborate Swazi pictures are a favourite with travellers. Even pottery painting has progressed from traditional earth colours to bright pinks, turquoise and gold. Black clay pots, known as "ludzino," are used for holding cereal beer, maize or corn.

Carving is another prominent handicraft. The two main materials used are wood and soapstone. In wood you will find stained bowls, animist masks and furniture. Soapstone allows the sculptor freedom in his work. Lovingly crafted figures, animals, 2 m high gods and busts are at their best along the King Mswati II Highway from Motshane to Pigg's Peak. Leatherwork is part of Swazi tradition. A livestock-herding people, they use hides for items such as sandals, bags and clothing.

Swazi print cloth is very attractive and can be used for clothing, table cloths etc. Carpets and tapestries can be found in the larger foreign-aided factories and workshops. Places of note for woven, knitted and hand-made curios are: Rosecraft near Malkerns, Mantenga Craft in the Swazi Plaza and Tishweshwe Crafts, north of Malkerns. Jewellery features prominently in Swazi tradition. Copper, beads, wood and glass are used in the manufacture of creations and designs that are unique to Swaziland.

Naturally, grasswork is also readily available. Baskets used as containers, mats for sleeping on and for traditional weddings, and bowls, are handmade from grass and sisal in the smallest of villages. Astute travellers will notice differences in the techniques and designs that are used in different parts of Swaziland. One form of grasswork that is recommended is the "sitja" bowl. Made from long threads of sisal and dyed in a variety of modern colours, these bowls make beautiful gifts or keepsakes.

As modernisation reaches out to touch even the remotest valley settlements, the traditional handicrafts are beginning to lose their appeal to the younger generation. To prevent a total loss of traditional skills, a Government Handicrafts Department has been set up to organise, manage and run handicraft training programmes. At the National Handicrafts Centre in the Ezulwini valley, intensive traditional skills training is offered. Students enrol for courses and receive both practical instruction in handicraft techniques, and lectures on business, marketing and economics.

It is highly unlikely that any visitor to Swaziland will return home without at least one memento or gift. Many tribal art experts consider Swaziland the most artistically creative country in Africa, something that all visitors will see for themselves.

Protect fragile items in your luggage by carefully packing clothing around them. Keep soapstone shiny and attractive by polishing the work with ordinary wax floor polish. Check the item before paying for it as often errors are only discovered later.

Soapstone animals may be unbalanced, displayed on an angled piece of wood. Find a flat patch of ground and check its straightness. The problem is easy to fix and will not take the sculptor more than a few minutes to rectify.

Traditional weapons and items of historical significance are not allowed across borders without written permission from the appropriate Swazi and South African government departments. Flora and fauna too need official clearance. Cycads, ferns, banana herbs and aloes are all expressly forbidden. With the abundance of flora in Swaziland many people are tempted to smuggle seeds or small plants out of the country. If caught, there is not only confiscation and a hefty fine, but also the likelihood of having to spend time in either the squalor of a Swazi prison or the bleakness of a South African gaol.

LANGUAGE

While it is possible to get around Swaziland with English, it is always better to know at least a few words of Siswati. In the cities, English is the lingua franca in hotels, banks, post offices, government services, hospitals and most schools. Even in isolated villages there will be at least one person who can understand and communicate in passable English. In the central and north-eastern Lebombo mountains, along the Mozambique border, Portuguese is understood and spoken by many in the mountain settlements. In the south-eastern Lebombos, Zulu is understood.

Where is the Tourist Office? – Likuphi Lihovisi Letivakashi?
Where is the hotel? – Likuphi ihotela?
Where is the post office? – Likuphi Eposini?
Where is the bus/taxi? – Kukuphi ibhasi/ithekisi?
Hello, how are you? – Sawubona, unjani?
I am well. – Ngikhona.
Good-bye. – Hamba Kahle (Go well); Sala Kahle (Stay well)
Thank you. – Ngiyabonga.

3 GETTING THERE

AIR

Overseas visitors flying in will have to first fly either to Johannesburg in South Africa or to Maputo in Mozambique. From South Africa flights are available on Royal Swazi National Airways, which has six flights per week. Airlink operates Monday, Tuesday, Wednesday, Friday and Sunday from the port city of Durban. Comair has a three days a week schedule from Johannesburg. From Mozambique, Linhas Aereas de Mocambique goes to Swaziland five times per week. Advance bookings are suggested for these airlines. Royal Swazi National Airways, P.O. Box 1521, Mbabane, Swaziland. Tel. (09268) 43486/7, fax 45984. Linhas Aereas de Mocambique, P.O. Box A403, Swazi Plaza, Swaziland. Tel. (09268) 44782, fax 45411. Airlink, P.O. Box 7529, Bonaero Park, 1622. Tel. (011) 973-2941. Comair, P.O. Box 7015, Bonaero Park, 1622. Tel. (011) 921-0222.

Royal Swazi Airways offers several air-hotel tour packages to Swaziland from South Africa. Prices are reasonable and accommodation is at tourist-class hotels and inns.

Visitors who are travelling through other southern African countries can take airlines from there directly to Swaziland. Lesotho Airways departs for Swaziland from Moshoeshoe Airport near Maseru on a Saturday. Reservations can be made telephonically: tel. (09266) 312453. Leaving Harare on Tuesday, Air Zimbabwe goes to Matsapha airport in Swaziland. For more details telephone them in Zimbabwe: (09263) 14-737011. Finally, from the capital of Botswana, Gabarone, Air Botswana departs for Swaziland at 14h15 on a Sunday. Contact Air Botswana, P.O. Box 92, Gabarone, Botswana. Tel. (09267) 352812/35, fax 374802. Note that an airport tax is charged in Swaziland.

OVERLAND

Travelling to Swaziland overland from Europe is an unusual and exciting way of reaching the country. With the road tarred all the way from Kenya through Tanzania, Zambia, Zimbabwe and South Africa, Nairobi has become a starting point for many travellers and tours.

For almost 4 740 km this good road passes through some of the most spectacular countries on the African continent. From the famous game parks of southern Kenya, through Tanzania and the breathtaking Masai Plateau, it continues on into the dense bush of Zambia to Victoria Falls. South Africa, sold as a land of beauty and splendour, will satisfy whatever it is the tourist wants in the way of visiting Africa.

Hitchhiking from Kenya to Swaziland is possible. The time you have available decides your journey's duration. It can be done in a week. But this is not the way to undertake an African odyssey. Give yourself at least two months to appreciate what you see and experience. Public transport is another way of reaching Swaziland. While inter-state buses do run across entire countries in one trip, you should rather consider making a series of "hops" to reach Swaziland. In Nairobi, many buses and taxis leave for the Kenya-Tanzania border at Namanga. Get to the bus depot on Accra and Cross Roads by 6h00. Taking one of these early buses will have you in Tanzania before midday. From 5h00 to 18h00, buses leave from Arusha to Dodoma. At Dodoma you may have to spend the night or try hitchhiking. Buses depart for the Tanzania-Zambia border, Tunduma, on Monday, Wednesday, Friday, Saturday and Sunday. If you are in a hurry, take a taxi south to Iringa. From Iringa, catch any of the four daily buses that run from Dar es Salaam to Mbeya and back. The estimated time from Iringa to the border is about 10 hours. Getting through Zambia entails crossing the border at Mpulungu, then taking one of the regular buses to Kasama. It's easy then finding a bus to Lusaka. Numerous buses and taxis follow the route to Victoria Falls and the Zimbabwe border. Catch the bus which leaves Lusaka daily at 10h00 and takes about seven hours to reach Bulawayo. At the bus station on Lobengula Street in Bulawayo, travellers will find buses leaving for the South African border, about 322 km away. Long-distance buses are also available from Harare direct to Johannesburg. There are buses from the sleepy South African town of Messina to Pretoria: one departs at around 5h00. The trip takes about four and a half hours. There are daily departures of buses to Swaziland from outside Pretoria Station at the top end of Paul Kruger Street. They leave for the Oshoek border post and take about five hours.

TO AND FROM SOUTH AFRICA

There are 12 official border posts through which people arriving from South Africa may enter Swaziland. The one most frequently used is Oshoek/Ngwenya on the road from the major South African cities of

Johannesburg and Pretoria. Another much-used entry point is in the south through Golela/Lavumisa.

These directions describe getting to Swaziland either from the Witwatersrand (Johannesburg/Pretoria), or the port city of Durban. Getting to Swaziland from Cape Town will involve first travelling to Johannesburg.

From Pretoria, take the N4 national road east. Stay on this dual carriageway past Bronkhorstspruit (about 50 km) and Witbank (98 km). Approximately 5 km east of the coal-mining town of Witbank, the N4 is joined by the R22 (also known as the N12) from the west-south-west. The dual highway bypasses Middelburg, an agricultural and coal mining centre. About another 45 km east, is a turn-off to the right along the R33 tarred road. Take this road to Carolina, which is 38 km south-east. Continue on the R33 through Carolina for 41 km to where it joins the N17, south of the Tweespruit river. Turn left (east) onto the N17 and travel through forests, hills and farms for 58 km, to the Oshoek/Ngwenya border posts. The total distance from Pretoria is about 307 km, with an average travelling time of 3-3½ hours.

From Johannesburg, you can take the N12 through Benoni for 143 km, to where it joins the N4 from Pretoria. Alternatively, take the N17 past Boksburg and Brakpan to the industrial town of Springs, 44 km east of Johannesburg. Continue on the N17, skirting the South African Air Force radar station at Devon, past Leandra to Bethal, 145 km from Johannesburg. At Bethal you have the choice of going another 86 km along the R38 through Hendrina to Carolina or straight along the N17 to Ermelo. Stay on the N17 for approximately 36 km to Chrissiesmeer (where South Africa's largest inland fresh-water lake can be seen). From Chrissiesmeer it is another 82 km to the Oshoek/Ngwenya border. Total distance is around 320 km, the trip taking about four hours.

From the friendly harbour and holiday city of Durban, take the N2 national road north. This tarred road hugs the scenic north coast for about 182 km to the sugar growing area of Empangeni. Proceeding in a northerly direction, follow the N2 for 52 km into more sugar cane fields around Mtubatuba. From this village the N2 turns inland to pass the world famous wildlife sanctuaries of Umfolozi and Hluhluwe before plunging into rolling savanna and tribal settlements. About 94 km from Mtubatuba you will skirt Mkuze, where the first sight of the Lebombo mountains can be seen to the north. Staying on the N2, pass Candover on the shores of Pongolapoort dam (Josini dam), and continue 19 km north-west to the turning to Golela.

Golela is a small border hamlet, 9 km east from where the N2 becomes the R29. The approximate distance from Durban is 367 km. The travelling time is about 4-4½ hours.

Long-distance buses depart from Johannesburg to Mbabane five days a week. These trips take about eight hours. They leave from Johannesburg train station at 7h30, arriving at Mbabane around 15h30. Contact Transnet in South Africa, tel. (011) 7747606.

4 GETTING AROUND

TRAIN

Train enthusiasts will be disappointed if they hope to see Swaziland by train. Although there are almost 300 km of railroad in Swaziland there are no passenger services. Adventurous travellers have limited choices if they hope to catch trains. The one is to speak to the drivers or guards at the main railway junction in Matsapha. Reports continue to come through of visitors who have been fortunate enough to get train rides to various parts of the country.

Information on routes and time schedules can be obtained by writing to: Swaziland Railway, P.O. Box 475, Mbabane, Swaziland. Tel. (09268) 42486, fax 45009.

BUS

Travelling around Swaziland by bus is exciting and enlightening. The sights, smells, sounds and difficulties become part of the Swazi experience. There is an extensive system of bus services throughout the country. Services cover routes to even the most remote villages. Prices are low and the service regular.

Be prepared for some degree of discomfort should you decide to travel by bus. Buses are always crowded, usually slow with hard seats but do provide visitors the ideal opportunity for getting to meet Swazis. There is a choice of bus on the longer routes. For example, there are first and second class buses travelling from Lavumisa to Mbabane. Whichever bus you choose, do not expect air conditioning or hostesses. First class leaves at 7h30 and takes about four hours. Second class buses leave in the heat of the day and may take up to six hours to reach the capital.

Four buses per day arrive in Manzini from the Lomahasha border post. Once again there are classes. First class leaves Lomahasha at 9h00 and 13h00, taking about three hours to reach Manzini. Second class buses depart at 10h00 and 14h30, arriving in Manzini a minimum of four hours later. Regular buses serve the district towns and villages. It is possible to reach Mbabane or Manzini from any border crossing by taking the bus but it may involve a series of rides.

Discomfort goes with bus travel in Swaziland. Music is always played at ear splitting levels, and it is no use complaining, the volume will not be turned down. After a while, however, you will find that the music fades further into the background as you strike up conversations with fellow passengers. Plan a strategy for boarding the buses. If you are alone, pay a child to board the bus as it arrives at the depot. He will quickly find you a suitable seat and hold it until you finally manage to get through the crush onto the bus. If there are two or more of you, let the others hold the luggage while one person clambers on unencumbered and secures seats by placing a cloth or other easily identifiable object on them. Whatever you do, avoid getting a seat over the wheels or right at the front or back.

Large bus depots can be confusing. The best method of finding a bus to your particular destination is to enquire of the street vendors who are always found at bus stations. They have a good knowledge of which bus goes where, when and the cost. To make sure, ask the driver, his assistant and several of the passengers.

Luggage is strapped to the roof of buses amidst boxes, livestock, fresh produce and machinery. Check that nothing is dumped on top of your pack and that it has been securely fastened. For added security, padlock a length of chain to the carrier and your bags. At stops along the way items are simply thrown off and it is not uncommon for a visitor's bag to also sail off and out of sight. If visiting Swaziland during the wet season, take a large sheet of plastic with which to cover your luggage on the roof.

Should you decide to travel through Swaziland this way, be prepared for a real adventure. You will be drawn into the lives of the Swazi; sharing their meals, laughing, talking and experiencing Africa as it is lived by the people themselves. It will not be easy and you will require patience and good humour, but ultimately, it is the best way of visiting the country and mixing with the people.

MINIBUS TAXI

All minibus taxis are privately owned. Unlike neighbouring South Africa and Mozambique, there are relatively few minibus taxis in Swaziland. They can be found travelling the following routes: Ngwenya-Mbabane-Manzini-Big Bend-Lavumisa.

Nhlangano-Manzini.
Manzini-Lomahasha.
Mbabane-Hhohho.

Minibus taxis are faster, but more expensive and dangerous than buses. Saloon car taxis are also available from the country centres. Taking these usually involves negotiating the fee with the driver. One way of reducing this cost is by sharing the vehicle with other travellers.

Minibus taxis do not run to any fixed schedule, departing when the driver feels he has enough passengers. This can be discouraging to those with limited time. One solution is to inform the driver that you plan to catch his taxi, tell him where you will be, then go off and explore the town, returning every 15 minutes or so to check on passenger numbers in the vehicle. There will be an additional fee for luggage. These minibus taxis take no notice of signs indicating the maximum permissible passengers. Count on at least 20 adults. This excludes children and luggage which are also crammed in. If you plan to stick to the main roads, then minibus taxis should be considered. They are usually found at the same sites as buses, starting their day at about 7h00, and doing the last trip no later than 16h00.

AIR

Subsidised by the Swaziland government, Royal Swazi National Airways Corporation operates several flights a week both around Swaziland and to other destinations in southern Africa. Scan Air Charter provides light aircraft which can be chartered for tour flights of Swaziland or to specific locations within the country. Both fleets have expanded in recent years, more to generate income from the rapidly expanding industrial trade than from tourism.

Tickets can be pre-booked prior to arriving, but this is seldom necessary and it is quicker and easier to book your flight at the Matsapha airport near Manzini or at the offices in Mbabane. Foreign visitors buying air tickets in Swaziland are required to pay in cash or with an internationally accepted credit card. Be prepared with a book or "walkman"; delays are frequent both prior to departure and on arrival. Information regarding flights, departure and arrival times can be obtained from the operators. This information should only be used as a guide.

Royal Swazi National Airways

Physical address: Swazi Plaza, Mbabane, or at Matsapha Airport.
Postal address: P.O. Box 1521, Mbabane, Swaziland.
Telephone: (09268) 43486/7, fax 45984.

Scan Air Charter

Physical address: Matsapha Airport.
Postal address: P.O. Box 1231, Manzini, Swaziland.
Telephone: (09268) 84474, fax 84331.

OWN VEHICLE

This is the way that most visitors travel in Swaziland. Road conditions are generally good. Even on gravel district roads, it is possible for saloon cars to make the journey during the dry months. When exploring by foot, leave your vehicle at an hotel or with the RSP (police).

Knowledge of the care and maintenance of your vehicle is not as important as in less developed southern African countries – notably Lesotho and Botswana. Repairs can be carried out in all urban centres and in most rural centres. While labour costs are relatively cheap, prices of spares are outrageous. Obviously the ability to change a tyre or fan belt is necessary. This becomes vital if you go off the tarred roads onto the narrow and stone-strewn bush roads.

Take along a few emergency items: spare tyre, puncture repair kit, footpump, fuses and globes, plus some tools. Avoid driving at night; livestock on the road could cause accidents. Driving over weekends can also be dangerous, especially if you use major roads. There are an amazing number of drunk drivers in Swaziland. Try to get off the main routes and onto the gravel roads which link rural areas. People who can only visit Swaziland over a weekend, should consider doing the described southern route, which traverses mostly country roads.

During the wet season, anything less than a 4x4 vehicle is useless for country roads. It is alright to use a saloon car along tarred roads, but once onto gravel, you will need all the traction and power you have to cross swollen rivers, climb slippery hills and traverse mud-filled valleys.

Whatever you do while driving through Swaziland, observe the speed limit and drive with extreme caution. Traffic officers are incredibly harsh on foreign offenders. An instant cash settlement is demanded or you may be locked up and your vehicle impounded until the money is paid. In built up areas, cities, towns and villages the speed limit is 60 km/h. On the open road, between urban development, the maximum is 80 km/h. Buses and minibus taxis seem immune to speed regulations. It is not unusual to find a bus hurtling along at well over 120 km/h between Manzini and Big Bend, or from Pigg's Peak to Mbabane.

Being such a small country, it is quite easy to drive across Swaziland in a relatively short time. Fuel is available at many towns and villages. With the high population, these are seldom more than 20 km apart. Approximate distances for the main routes are:

Oshoek-Mbabane: 20 km
Mbabane-Manzini: 39 km
Manzini-Big Bend: 79 km
Big Bend-Lavumisa: 73 km
Manzini-Malkerns: 20 km
Matsapha-Nhlangano: 90 km
Nhlangano-Mahamba: 18 km
Manzini-Siteki: 66 km
Manzini-Lomahasha: 109 km
Oshoek-Pigg's Peak: 56 km
Pigg's Peak-Matsamo: 95 km

Two car rental organisations, Avis and Hertz/Imperial, have facilities in Swaziland. Both have centres in Mbabane and Manzini and at Matsapha airport. Car hire is expensive and something of a luxury for most visitors. Charges are made per day and per kilometre – this quickly adds up if exploring the country. As these two companies are international, it is possible to drop off the vehicle beyond Swaziland's borders. Naturally, there is a high fee for this service. Prior bookings can be made directly from your home country's Avis or Hertz offices. In Swaziland contact: Avis Rent-a-Car, P.O. Box 31, Manzini. Tel. 52137. At Matsapha Airport, tel. 52734, fax 52735. Hertz/Imperial Rent-a-Car, Swazi Plaza, Mbabane. Tel. 43486. At Matsapha airport, tel. 84393, fax 84396.

MOTORCYCLE

This is arguably one of the best modes of transport for a visit to Swaziland. To feel the wind, smell the earthy scents and stop where and whenever you like is a definite advantage. In the far eastern Lebombo mountains scrambler-type motorbikes will be able to get to secluded mountain villages and settlements where there are no roads. The disadvantage is that security becomes a major concern. Leave your motorcycle unattended for longer than two minutes and something is bound to be pilfered. Leave it chained up in a hotel parking lot or with the RSP (police), take the luggage off and store it.

Motorcycles are a rarity in Swaziland and you are unlikely to meet other motorcyclists. Because of this, finding a place which can do repairs is difficult. Be capable of carrying out your own minor repairs on the roadside. A comprehensive tool kit and bag of spares is important if you plan to go off-road in the remote regions. Include spare tubes (front and back), blow-weld temporary puncture repair compound, puncture kit, footpump, master-links, spokes, fuses, globes and accelerator, clutch and brake cables. Throw in a workshop manual just in case. Before leaving for a motorcycle trip through Swaziland, give your bike a thorough service, changing any sprockets, chains or cables necessary. Spares can be ordered in Swaziland, but the wait can prove too long. Contact: Carson Wheels, tel. 52466.

HITCHHIKING

Hitchhiking is a fun way of exploring Swaziland. Not only is it very cheap, but also easy. The opportunity to encounter the whole spectrum of Swazi culture is an added attraction. Along the main routes hitchhikers will hardly ever have to wait for more than 10 minutes before someone stops. In the rural areas almost every car that passes will offer you a ride. Around the heavily populated urban centres, most drivers will expect payment. Make sure to sort this out prior to accepting the lift. On gravel district roads traffic is infrequent. To be certain of getting a lift, be on the road by 7h00 and never after 17h00. A pleasant alternative is to combine walking and hitchhiking.

Over weekends the traffic flow increases from Friday afternoon to a peak on Saturday evening. All day on Sunday there is a steady flow of private transport in the opposite direction. Between Mbabane and Manzini hitch hikers may have to literally jump in front of an approaching vehicle. The driver will stop and, with a huge grin and exclamations as to your courage, offer you a lift.

Unfortunately, caution needs to be exercised as to whom you accept a lift from. Women travellers need to be especially wary. Many of the drivers will be drunk and driving recklessly to show off. Should you get into one of these vehicles by mistake, ask to be put out as soon as possible.

If hitchhiking in the wet summer months, be sure to have a poncho with which to cover yourself – many lifts are in open-back trucks.

Good places to hitch from are: Oshoek border to Mbabane; outside the hospital in Mbabane for lifts to Manzini; anywhere on the road to Malkerns; from the Manzini Club in Manzini for lifts to Big Bend, Siteki or Lomahasha; at the turn-off to the King Mswati II Highway near Motshane for north-western Swaziland; at Mahamba for lifts to Nhlangano; in front of the fresh produce market in Lavumisa for lifts to Big Bend. Hitch hiking from Matsapha to Hlatikulu or Nhlangano can be difficult. Walk about 4 km east of Matsapha, to the turn-off for Nhlangano. All vehicles travelling this road will wind through the spectacular Grand Valley.

BICYCLE

Because of the vast number of hill and mountain ranges which make up Swaziland, there are few bicycles in the country. Those that you see will be in cities or large towns. In country districts, only headmen own bicycles as status symbols. To bicycle around Swaziland will be frustrating, challenging, exciting and unforgettable.

As towns and even cities are small by Western standards, pedalling about viewing sights is limited. Still, occasionally people report having seen foreigners on bicycles in Swaziland. Taking a bicycle to Swaziland will be fraught with problems. Only the most basic spares are available, and then only in Mbabane or Manzini. This means that all tubes, tools, puncture kits, spokes, pumps, derailleur parts and cables need to be carried somewhere on the bike. Officials at the Swazi border posts are strangely suspicious of cyclists. There is no logical explanation for this, but cyclists are nearly always thoroughly searched when arriving or departing. In rural communities, you will be plagued by men who want to buy your bicycle. Getting them to understand how valuable it is to you as a mode of transport will have no effect. Eventually, out of desperation, you will probably get on your cycle and leave.

TOURS

For visitors who enjoy a vacation planned and arranged by someone else, Swaziland offers three tour operators. There are several which run tours from South Africa into Swaziland, but these are always expensive and the trip rushed.

Eco-Africa Safaris run tours which specialise in the natural beauty of Swaziland. Their aim is to foster an understanding of the natural world in all participants. Accommodation and service are of the highest standard, unsurpassed by any other tour operator in the country. Prices are fairly high, but the experience and knowledge that you gain will be well worth the cost. Popular, with a year-long clientele, Eco-Africa Safaris suggest that tourists make reservations at least three months in advance. The operation is run from the private and beautiful Phophonyane Lodge. Accommodation is in cottages and tented camps within the depths of natural forest, alongside a highland river.

Address: Eco-Africa Safaris, P.O. Box 199, Pigg's Peak, Swaziland.
Telephone: (09268) 71319, fax 44246.

Swaziland Safaris/African Camping Safaris run trips for adventurous visitors. Each tour is planned for a particular party, meaning that seldom are two visits ever the same. This is the cheapest and most laid-back tour outfit in Swaziland. There is no rush to reach sites. Days are long and lazy, with guests having time to do some of their own exploring. The whole concept behind this company is the enforced "African time" attitude. By the end of the journey, not only will you be relaxed, healthy and content, but your understanding and appreciation of the Swazi people will have increased as well. Book in advance for these tours. Try and get a group together, which will keep the overall costs down and give you all some great memories.

Address: Swaziland Safaris/African Camping Safaris, P.O. Box 1240, Mbabane, Swaziland.
Telephone: (09268) 44522, fax 44246.

Royal Swazi National Airways Corporation offer tourist packages from Johannesburg (South Africa) to Matsapha. Included in the high cost are: flight, accommodation and breakfasts. Should you choose their Forester's Arms option, a hired car is included. Packages range from two to seven nights. Accommodation is provided in six of the top hotels in Swaziland: Mountain Inn, Pigg's Peak Hotel and Casino, Royal Swazi Sun Hotel and Casino, Forester's Arms, Ezulwini Sun or Lugogo Sun. There is not a great demand for these tours, even though rebates for children under 18 and families are offered. Contact the Royal Swazi Airways offices in South Africa for reservations.

Address: Royal Swazi National Airways, Budget Rent-a-Car House, Main Street, Johannesburg.
Telephone: (011) 3319467/8, fax 3316918.

Umhlanga Tours is the oldest and most experienced tour operator in Swaziland. Itineraries include half day, full day and specialised trips. It's rather pointless going on a half day tour of Swaziland. Visitors should join one of the longer tours which include such sights as Swaziland's big game parks and Swaziland by night. This is another tour operator that offers tourists the chance to stay and eat at Swaziland's best hotels, restaurants and inns. Visits to casinos are included in the tour. Prices vary depending on the tour and its length. Whichever you choose, rest assured that it will be expensive, with additional expenses that you have to carry. One trip that is highly recommended, despite the cost, is the night game drive in the Mlilwane Game Sanctuary. Visitors with limited knowledge about the behaviour of wildlife in the African bush should not miss this short but informative wilderness drive. You should be able to get onto a tour on the evening of departure, but Umhlanga Tours prefers reservations with deposits.

Address: (Postal) Umhlanga Tours, P.O. Box 2197, Mbabane, Swaziland. (Physical) Swazi Plaza, Mbabane.
Telephone: (09268) 45222, fax 44246.

5 MBABANE

Mbabane is the capital of Swaziland and the largest city in the country. Busy and aggressive, it is a city in transition. Construction, road works and over-population makes this one of the most congested cities on the continent. Nestled under the Dlangeni hills, Mbabane – which means "something bitter" – was founded in about 1902 by the British colonial administration. Government offices, embassies, travel agents, top-class hotels and numerous international banks are located in and around the capital.

A word of warning: crime, usually of a violent nature, is a serious problem in Mbabane. Never walk around the streets alone at night, nor even during the day if you are a white woman on your own. Keep to the main thoroughfares of Gilfillan and Allister Miller Roads. Muggings, rapes, robberies, hold-ups and abductions are becoming commonplace in Mbabane. At night, gangs of armed youths cruise the streets. Eager for some action, their targets are frequently unprotected and money-carrying tourists. It is however probably no worse than any other inner city anywhere in the world. Be practical: do not walk around the market area after dark or pull out a wallet full of cash when someone asks you for lilangeni down an alley. Try and act as though you know where you are going. Rather than spend time in the capital, quickly complete any business you need to do and get as far away as possible.

Mbabane is a cosmopolitan city: lively, interesting, pleasantly landscaped and a good place to get essential business and bureaucratic matters sorted out. As in other African cities, there is a shortage of housing and vast differences between the classes. This is obvious between working-class and shanty areas of town and middle-class suburbs with spacious mansions and manicured gardens. If you make Swazi acquaintances, get them to take you on a tour of the working-class and shanty areas, where visitors will see the entire spectrum of Swazi life.

INFORMATION

Tourist information is obtainable at one of the better staffed and equipped tourist offices in southern Africa. The staff are attentive, knowledgeable and fluent in English. City and country maps are available free. A small

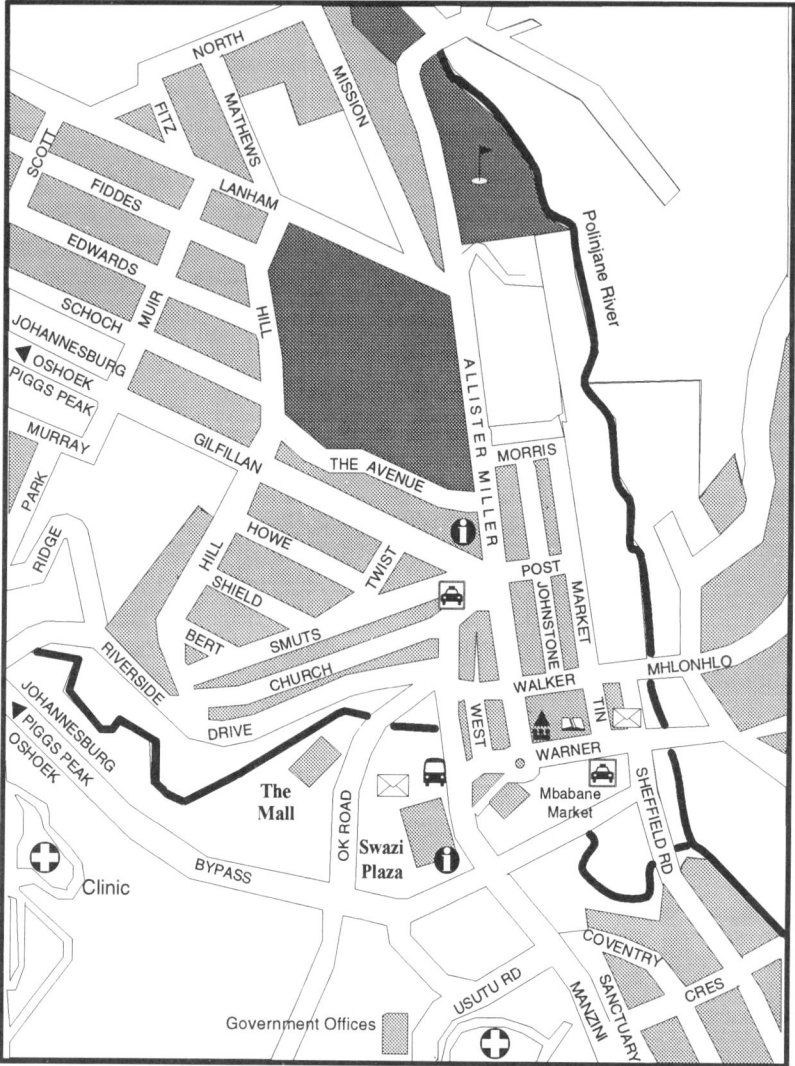

but comprehensive display of books and curios is also available. Although the main office is in Gilfillan Road, another, more informative office, is situated in the Swazi Plaza, between the Mbabane bypass and market. Ask for a copy of *What's On*. This free publication includes details on local restaurants, cinemas, places to visit and tourist shopping. Numerous excursions and tours can be arranged through the tourist office, as well as hotel accommodation. It is frequently very busy and visitors should get there at opening time, which is usually around 8h30 on weekdays.

The post office is on Msunduza Road near the impressive town council building. Mail can be sent to the poste restante here. Ask at the enquiries counter for the box containing all the mail. Nothing is in alphabetical order and visitors will have to spend a while going through the gigantic box (some letters have postmarks from the 1970s). International telephone calls can also be made from here; contact the postmaster who will show you to a drab yellow room with a desk and telephone. Link-ups are instantaneous and far more reliable and cheaper than trying to do it through one of the luxury hotels.

Several international banks have branches in Swaziland, all of which are experienced in dealing with travellers cheques, guaranteed bank cheques, credit cards and hard currency exchanges. The best place for getting finances sorted out is at the Union bank in the Swazi Plaza. Many top-class hotels in Mbabane and the Ezulwini valley will change travellers cheques; but their handling charges are high. A thriving black market exists in the Mbabane market, but beware of the RSP (police), who regard illegal dealing in foreign currency very seriously.

Fuel is available at filling stations throughout the capital and surrounding areas. Check that bowser settings are back on zero before pumping begins. Many fuel stations have differing petrol prices. This is something of a mystery to many visitors. No logical explanation is offered, but make full use of the lower prices. One garage worth trying is on the corner of Gilfillan and Allister Miller Streets.

Hitchhiking into and out of Mbabane is a nightmare. Suburbs begin far out of town, which means that unless you are dropped in the CBD it is almost impossible to reach the city centre. On arrival, it is best to ask your lift to take you to the Swazi Plaza on the Mbabane bypass or to the RSP (police) near the corner of Market and Mhlonhlo Streets. To leave, take a minibus taxi or bus to the outskirts of the city. Only get off once clear of the main suburbs. Using public transport is a pleasure in comparison to hitchhiking. The main bus and minibus taxi depot is behind the Swazi Plaza and in front of the Mbabane market. It is an area of noise, colour, people, fumes and a traveller's delight. It is also the best place from which to commence exploring the city. For detailed information on destinations and times for public transport, ask any of the street vendors that sell around the bus stop. Foreign visitors seldom use public transport from Mbabane and it is a fascinating experience answering the questions that passengers ask, as you wait in long queues. This bus stop is where travellers will find buses or taxis bound for all districts of the kingdom.

PLACES TO EAT

Mbabane has several international restaurants and hotel dining rooms. Expect to pay high prices for meals, which are invariably excellent. The following are recommended:

La Casserole: German and continental cuisine, The Mall. Tel. 46426.

Marco's Trattoria: Traditional Italian menu, Allister Miller Street. Tel. 45029.

Hwa Li Restaurant: The finest Chinese restaurant in Swaziland, Dhlan'ubeka House. Tel. 45986.

Lourenco Marques: Spicy seafood and provincial Portuguese dishes, Gilfillan Street. Tel. 43097.

Fast foods can be bought from American-style menus throughout the city. The Longhorn Takeaway at the Swazi Plaza is really good and reasonably priced. Pablo's Takeaway next to the Jabula Inn gives an impression of efficiency and cleanliness until you decide to order. While Pablo's has tasty food, low prices and modern decor, it falls down hopelessly in customer service. Their Sunday lunch buffet is well priced and enormous. There may not be a large variety of dishes, but the eat-as-much-as-you-like offer will be a boon to budget travellers.

For the adventurous, there are numerous street vendors and suburban eating establishments. Tasty and traditional snacks and light meals can be bought from the hawkers who sell at the Mbabane bus depot and Mbabane market. From porridge and herb chicken to the original goat's head soup, most visitors will find something to appease their hunger. Near the clinic on St Michael's Road, women sell hot bread, thick beef stew and sliced fresh tomatoes. Vegetarians will find a wide selection of fresh produce outside the Mbabane market. Depending on the season, you can purchase mangoes, tomatoes, potatoes, sweet corn, corn on the cob and that most trivial of decorations, parsley. Bargaining is frowned upon at the fresh produce stalls within the market, but across the car park and under the trees, equally good fresh produce can be bought after a protracted bargaining session. The best way to set a lower price is to visit the produce stalls outside the Swazi Plaza, The Mall (Emphalwini) and in the market. Armed with this knowledge, make your offer to the street vendors. Do not be ridiculous; what some visitors spend on a meal is a two month salary to many of these people.

PLACES TO STAY

Very few visitors actually stay in Mbabane, which has little in the way of attractions. With the close proximity of the beautiful Ezulwini valley, most tourists stay there. Accommodation is available in town but be prepared for high tariffs and mediocre service. The majority of guests at establishments in Mbabane are usually businessmen.

The Tavern: High tariff

In the middle of town on Allister Miller Street, The Tavern caters primarily to business conferences and salesmen. With good views, an extensive menu, often rude staff and noisy locals, the hotel is a paradox. Some guests return again and again, while you are just as likely to meet those who cannot wait to leave. Ironically, it always seems to be full. Whether all the people milling about in the foyer are guests, revellers, relatives or staff is quite unknown. Accommodation is in 32 rooms, with en suite bathrooms. For visitors who intend staying for a longer period, a fully furnished self-catering flat is available. Meals can be taken either at "The Hatch" pub or in the Jubilee Restaurant. Reservations for rooms are required at least 30 days ahead.

Address: The Tavern, P.O. Box 25, Mbabane, Swaziland.
Telephone: (09268) 42361

Jabula Inn: High tariff

Also in the city, the Jabula Inn is tucked in behind an avenue of trees on Allister Miller Street. Next door is Pablo's Takeaways. This inn is in an ideal position for visiting businessmen who need access to the city centre with its office blocks, government institutions and financial houses. Accommodation is provided in 23 comfortable double rooms all with their own bathroom. The cosy Pele Pub is a lunch time favourite with city office workers who stream in for the cheap and delicious pub lunch. A small disco, the Galaxy, is enjoyable most nights of the week, but really raves on Friday and Saturday evenings. There is a slightly older crowd at this nightclub and you are as likely to meet a company director as a postman. Aside from offering a central position within easy walking distance of many shopping centres – such as the Swazi Plaza and Mbabane market – numerous activities can be arranged from the inn. Golf, tennis and bowls are available at the Mbabane Club across the road from Coronation Park. It is advisable that reservations are made.

Address: Jabula Inn, P.O. Box 15, Mbabane, Swaziland.
Telephone: (09268) 42043 or 42406, fax 45855.

Budget travellers may find it difficult getting suitable accommodation in Mbabane. Unless you manage to get lodgings with a Mbabane family, most people head east into the Ezulwini valley where there are numerous cheap rooms and camping sites. However, if you must stay in the city, there are at least two places worth trying.

Mbabane Youth Centre, graded as low tariff, is a rendezvous for foreign-aid workers. Go west along Msunduza Road, past the post office. The centre is not in a particularly safe area and visitors should get there during daylight. If you arrive by public transport, telephone the centre on 42406. Sometimes they will send someone to meet you at the bus depot. There is always an interesting crowd of people at the centre. While you may be required to share dormitory accommodation, the experience and hints about travel through Swaziland are invaluable.

Another place worth trying for shoestring visitors is the old but comfortable Thokoza Church Mission. It is located off Mhlonhlo Road along Polinjane Road. The best way of finding it is to ask at the RSP (police) or the Roman Catholic church at the Y-junction east of the Mbabane River and Mhlonhlo Road. Contact them ahead of your arrival, tel. 46681. Run by an order of Mennonites, your religion is of no consequence to them. They are devout and genuine people, not out to convert the heathen, but to render whatever assistance is required. No fee is asked, but travellers should consider a donation based on what they would have expected to pay at a medium-low tariff facility. Spend time talking to these devotees. Their insight and understanding of the complexities which face Swaziland are fresh and thought provoking. On Friday evenings they are not averse to going to one of the local discos with visitors, and although they do not drink alcohol they do enjoy themselves. Young visitors looking for basic but clean accommodation should definitely stay at the Thokoza Church Mission.

THINGS TO SEE AND DO

Movies and theatre productions are popular in Mbabane. Four times per year theatre playgroups put on famous productions. These are usually sold out well before opening night. A few enterprising souls always buy extra tickets and tout them at the entrance prior to performances. Expect to pay a considerably higher price for these black market tickets. Get to the Theatre Club on Morris Road by at least 18h30 on the evening of a play if you hope to get tickets. Black-tie affairs are something that only happen at official functions and at the colonial Mbabane Club. Many of the younger theatregoers simply wear jeans and collared shirts.

Cinemas are also located in the city and are quite something. With pushing, tugging and shoving, the mass of people is borne forward to the ticket office. Once there, you must shout across the heads of less vocal and physical patrons. Being issued a ticket is no guarantee that you will actually get a seat. As the doors open, it is every person for themself. Having gained a seat, do not budge. Occasionally someone bigger than you may try and sit on you to good-naturedly get you to move. When you have seen the size of some of the Swazi women, it may be more prudent to swop around, with you sitting on her ample lap instead. It is all rather fun though and seldom does the situation ever turn ugly.

THINGS TO BUY

No visit to the capital is complete without a visit to the Mbabane market, behind the Swazi Plaza and across the Mbabane River. This is not a traditional tribal market as is found in Manzini. Prices are high, there is no real bargaining and you will encounter more foreigners than locals. However, for visitors who are looking for curios, there is a wide selection of handicrafts, clothing and other items on sale. Most of the goods are mass produced and lack the dedicated finishes that are found on goods at rural markets or at Manzini. Try to get there early in the morning, before 9h00 and the rush of coach tours.

Other places worth considering for curios are:

- African Fantasy, The Mall. Expensive and directed at the well-heeled tourist, there is a wide selection of curios ranging from grasswork to T-shirts.

- Indingilizi Art Gallery, Johnstone Street. Art works by local and foreign artists. A small restaurant is also available. Try their cream teas while sitting among the odd mix of tribal and western works on sale. For travellers who have not had the courage to eat at Swazi eating establishments, ask for one of the traditional Swazi meals here. There is little typically African art for sale anywhere in Mbabane, but here at least, there is a good selection of pieces on display. Prices are high for most goods, but the quality of workmanship is excellent and the animist masks are a definite buy.

- Living in Africa, Swazi Plaza. This is the ideal place for visitors who want high quality curios. The selection is bewildering, from small bead and shell Swazi earrings, to large decorative mats and table-cloths. If you cannot find a curio at Living In Africa then it is unlikely that you will find anything at all in Swaziland. Glasswork from various parts of the world have found their way to this little shop in the heart of Swaziland. Attractive, personalised gifts can be had by asking that names, designs or motifs be engraved onto local recycled glass products. Allow a few days for this to be done. Should visitors require a specific Swazi curio, every effort will be made by the management to accommodate you. Tel. (09268) 46468, fax 43021.

- Swazi Flame, Swazi Plaza. A small shop that has a fairly good choice of ethnic clothing, plus an interesting array of khaki safari clothing, leopard band hats and other colonial trinkets. Ivory is also sold at this shop, sometimes passed off as bone.

- Mantenga Craft, Swazi Plaza. A subsidiary of the large centre outside the Mantenga Falls Hotel, this shop has an impressive array of sisal baskets, handwoven rugs and bedspreads, glass animals and leather goods. Prices are high. Credit cards are accepted.

Mbabane is an enigma. It motivates, depresses, swirls with affluent life and weeps in shanty quarters. No visitor to this city will be unaffected. You will either love or hate it, but you will never feel indifferent. To many, it is merely a break on their journey into the interior. All across the capital are signs that Mbabane is aiming for its golden age. Construction is in progress everywhere. Modern glass skyscrapers push upwards but it will be in the poorer areas that you will see the truth about the city. Outwardly it prospers, inwardly it staggers under overpopulation and unemployment. Mbabane is an experience, not always enjoyed but always remembered.

6 EZULWINI VALLEY

Swaziland's answer to Turkey's Grand Bazaar is the almost 30 km stretch of valley between Mbabane and the turn-off for Malkerns. This area is the Ezulwini valley (the Valley of Heaven) and is a journey down a continuous tourist arcade. It is set in a magnificent valley through which the Mbabane river flows on its way to Matsapha dam.

Leaving Mbabane, travel south-east. Follow the road signs for the Casino and Manzini. The heavily used, well maintained tarred road climbs out of Mbabane through tree-lined avenues. For a good view of the capital, stop at the highest point on the road, above the housing estates. Cradled in a bowl of hills, the city looks like a mini-town from this height. There is a 60 km/h speed limit here and visitors would do well to adhere to the law. From the housing estates, travellers pass through what resembles a concrete doorway. In bold bright letters the announcement: Phuma Lankga Sikotse Long Live the King, tells all people that Swaziland is proudly a kingdom.

Then the road starts to descend Malagwane hill, which is sometimes swathed in thick mist. If at all possible, avoid this road during bad weather or the hours of darkness. Should you experience vehicle problems try and make it to one of the hotels or garages which are found every few hundred metres on the road from Mbabane to Lobamba (The Royal Village of the King.)
A mere 2 km from Mbabane is the Mountain Inn.

Mountain Inn: High-medium tariff

This inn is set in one of Swaziland's most beautiful locations. High above roads, forests and rivers, the Mountain Inn commands awesome views across Swaziland's hundreds of hills, and down into the Ezulwini valley. With a dedicated, cordial and highly trained staff, visitors will have considerable trouble finding a friendlier hotel along the road from Mbabane to Matsapha. Accommodation for guests is in 60 double rooms, all with en suite bathrooms, radio, telephone and television. House-cleaning staff are knowledgeable to the point where they can advise travellers on local points of interest. A luxurious cinema is available, as is a large pool. In the Friar Tuck restaurant an extensive menu and wine list caters to most tastes, including vegetarians. Breakfasts are taken on the second floor, in a serene setting overlooking the Ezulwini valley.

While the spacious conference centre attracts many business functions, it is in the bar that the real ambience of the Mountain Inn comes out. Warm, cosy, friendly and offering cheap, tasty pub lunches, travellers will meet not only foreigners but also locals.

Horse riding, walking excursions with either the Historical or Nature Society, and vehicle tours, can be arranged at reception. From porters to waitresses, gardeners to security men, the staff are committed to ensuring guests have a memorable and satisfying stay.

Reservations are necessary, but should you arrive unannounced, staff will endeavour to find you accommodation – even to the point of phoning other hotels in the area. It is recommended that you stay at least one night at the Mountain Inn.

Address: Mountain Inn, P.O. Box 223, Mbabane, Swaziland.
Telephone: (09268) 42781, fax 45393.

On clear days, the descent from the hills around Mbabane into the Ezulwini valley is a spectacular journey. Looking east, visitors will be able to see all the way across Swaziland to the Lebombo mountains which border Mozambique. Forests of conifers, gums and indigenous trees creep down to the very edge of the road, creating a cool and fragrant passage until the entrance to the Swazi Inn and Red Feather Restaurant.

Swazi Inn: High tariff

Tucked into the folds at the head of the Ezulwini valley, the Swazi Inn is about 3 km from Mbabane. It offers wonderful views, cottages, good service and an excellent menu in the Red Feather Restaurant. A number of tourist activities can be arranged through the hotel; these should be made at least 24 hours earlier. Being close to both the city and the nightlife of the Ezulwini valley hotels, the Swazi Inn could be attractive to middle-low budget travellers. Reservations here, as at all hotels in the Ezulwini valley, are necessary well ahead of arrival. Book at least 60 days ahead.

Address: Swazi Inn, P.O. Box 121, Mbabane, Swaziland.
Telephone: (09268) 42235.

South-east of the Swazi Inn, the road drops past Life Ministries of Swaziland. Camping and cheap accommodation can sometimes be found here. Leave a donation if you do use the facilities. Incredible views down through the valley can be seen from this point. Even though you can see buildings all along the route, the wide expanse of a blue heaven carries thoughts and visions above the crush of urbanisation.

Next is B.A. Dlamini Camp Site and Rest Rooms. No reservations are necessary, but you need to be desperate to stay here. It is close to the main road, there is no security, facilities are abominable and the tariff is ridiculously high. Occasionally, shoestring travellers may be forced to stay, but it is far better, not to mention safer, to ask for accommodation at Life Ministries of Swaziland. If you have no choice but to stay here, contact the manager at tel. 43655, so that he can open a rest room for you or show you where to camp in the overgrown jumble of grass, beer cans, papers and shattered trees.

Continuing down into the Ezulwini valley, travellers will encounter numerous lunatic drivers determined to overtake each other. Keep to the extreme left whenever possible. Their attitude and the consequences can be confirmed by glancing down into the smaller valleys off the main road. Wrecks of cars, trucks and buses litter many areas, mute testimony to the dangers of Swazi driving.

The Mgenule Motel and strictly halal Tandoori Restaurant offers visitors an opportunity to eat spicy Oriental dishes from a scrupulously clean establishment. Accommodation is comfortable, basic and relatively cheap. Not well known, this motel will soon be too popular to get reservations at. As yet, these are not necessary, but make a booking anyway.

Address: Mgenule Motel, P.O. Box 711, Mbabane, Swaziland.
Telephone: (09268) 61041, fax 46465.

Near the Mgenule Motel is the Timbali Caravan Park, part of Zulwini Holdings, and classed as medium to low tariff. Just 10 km south-east of Mbabane, this caravan site has additional accommodation in self-catering rondavals and good tent pitches with clean ablution facilities. The park is well situated for exploring the upper reaches of the valley and visiting the five star hotels and casinos along the route. Timbali Caravan Park is used by many budget travellers, families and, of course, caravanners. Avoid pitching your tent or parking your caravan too near the boundary fence. Instead, keep to the trees and rooms on the far side of the park. For camping, no prior reservation is required, but try and get there before 17h00. Visitors with caravans or those intending to stay in the rondavals, should apply in advance.

Address: Timbali Caravan Park, P.O. Box 1, Ezulwini, Swaziland.
Telephone: (09268) 61156.

Next to the caravan park is the legendary Calabash Continental Restaurant. Advertised as "A touch of the Black Forest in Swaziland," this is one restaurant where it is worth paying the high price of meals. If it were not for the fact that items of Swazi culture can be seen, it would be easy to imagine yourself in Europe instead of Africa. Attention to detail is obvious, as is the preparation of each plate of food. While Austrian, Swiss and German meals are on offer, try the German dishes in particular. Vegetarians should mention this fact on arrival. They can expect an equally varied choice and for some odd reason receive special service. It is difficult to just turn up and expect a table. Reservations are made weeks in advance, often from outside the country. Book well ahead by telephoning: (09268) 61187. Like most restaurants, the Calabash is closed on Mondays.

Further south-east, past the Islamic Institute, is Martin's Bar and Disco. This is a wild, boisterous and thoroughly enjoyable place to spend a weekend evening. Not many foreigners attend, but those that do can be sure of having a wonderful time. Arrive at about 22h30 on Friday or Saturday. The disco is always packed with locals and it can be difficult finding a seat. You will not be left alone for long; within minutes of arrival someone will ask you to join them on the dance floor, and then the evening really begins. The Swazis love dancing, and it will require some persuasion to get your partner to stop for a while. The disco carries on until sunrise.

Close to Midway Ka-Mkhulu Store and Mantenga Bottle Store is Thandabantu Roadhouse and Handicrafts. Curios are overpriced here but there is an excellent selection available. The attention to detail and pride in the pieces is enough incentive for tourists who stop and end up buying. While bargaining is not considered by most visitors, the vendors are prepared to negotiate prices. Particular works can also be ordered, but will take a few hours or days, depending on the size and detail involved. The clay and wooden objects on display are particularly attractive and make for small but uniquely Swazi gifts.

About 1,5 km from the handicraft stalls the road drops through a steep and well-wooded valley to the very expensive Swaziland Spa, Health and Beauty Studio. Treatments are extravagant and really relaxing. Mineral waters flow into a pool that has therapeutic benefits. Full body massages are available from highly qualified masseuses from 10h00-18h00 daily. From jacuzzi to modern gym, sauna to aromatherapy, it caters to all hedonists. Not many budget travellers or annual vacationers stop here for treatment, but those that do are pampered by well-trained, highly motivated and dedicated staff. If you can afford it, this is one place to spoil yourself with some form of personal attention. Bookings are essential.

Address: Swazi Spa, Health and Beauty Studio, P.O. Box 1455, Mbabane, Swaziland.
Telephone: (09268) 61164.

Further on, splendid views of the valley and surrounding peaks can be seen. Next is the famous Royal Swazi Sun Hotel, Casino and Country Club. A Shell garage precedes the establishment.

Royal Swazi Sun Hotel, Casino and Country Club: High tariff

This is Swaziland's shrine to the god Bacchus. Swaziland's reason-for-entry for many years, especially for South Africans, the Royal Swazi Sun is still paradise for many tourists. You will not find budget travellers here, nor inefficient staff or poor housekeeping. This is where the power of tourist dollars has created a never-never land of casinos, restaurants, cinemas, bars and recreational activities. For travellers who have been on the road for some time, this is one hotel that should be tried for total battery recharging.

The Royal Swazi Sun never sleeps; throughout the 24 hours something is happening. The hotel is not only gambling, revelry and x-rated movies though. Set on the charming wooded slopes of the Ezulwini valley, it is well situated for excursions to nearby Mlilwane Wildlife Sanctuary and the attractions along the road to Lobamba and Malkerns. Accommodation is in 122 of the most exquisite double rooms found anywhere in the kingdom. A dining room and three à la carte restaurants cater to virtually every taste. Golfers arrive from around the world to tackle the magnificent and demanding 18-hole golf course tucked in beneath the gentle Mdzimba hills. Tennis, squash, bowls and swimming are all provided in plush and peaceful surroundings.

Tourists will not only find this the ideal place in which to relax and be pampered, but also a place where the petty problems of travel can be forgotten for a while. It is easy to imagine that you have wandered into a dream world here. Even a Barclay's Bank is located on site to deal with visitors requests. This is probably the best bank at which to carry out foreign exchanges. The staff are well versed in the idiosyncrasies of international finance. Service is fast, accurate and efficient. Travellers passing this way should consider foregoing the chaos of banks in Mbabane and Manzini and do their deals at Barclays Bank here.

Then, of course, there is the casino. The lure for most guests at some stage of their stay, there are always people playing. Over weekends it can get crowded, but this just adds to the excitement. Slot machines are the most popular. Away from the rows of hackers, the serious gamblers are to be found at the quiet and sophisticated gaming tables. This area is not for people in jeans and sneakers. Formal dress is expected and the ability to squander money is required.

Do not expect to arrive unannounced at the Royal Swazi Sun Hotel, Casino and Country Club. Reservations are required and demanded of all guests. Even if you cannot afford to stay at the hotel, spend a few hours drifting through the establishment or having a light meal at the poolside.

Address: Royal Swazi Sun Hotel, Casino and Country Club, P.O.
             Box 412, Mbabane, or Private Bag, Ezulwini, Swaziland.
Telephone: (09268) 61001, fax 61606.

East of the Royal Swazi Sun is the 202-roomed Lugogo Sun Hotel. Between the two hotels is Thishewene Handicrafts. Aimed exclusively at the top drawer hotel trade, visitors will find items overpriced. Rather wait until you have travelled further into the country before making any large purchases. They can usually be found at least 40 per cent cheaper elsewhere. Relatively few of the goods are made locally, so shoppers also pay transport costs on their purchases.

Lugogo Sun Hotel: High tariff

With the largest accommodation in Swaziland, the Lugogo Sun Hotel is aimed at well-heeled tourists and tour groups. The atmosphere is less formal than at the Royal Swazi Sun, but do not be deceived into thinking that sport shorts and T-shirts are normal wear. Numerous business conferences are held here annually. Over weekends, outdoor grills, Swazi tribal dancing and games are held. You will encounter more families staying at the Lugogo than at Royal Swazi. Its appeal to families is the hotel's main selling strength. Rooms are all air-conditioned, with bathroom, telephone, radio and television including a video channel.

A bus ferries guests to and fro between the casinos of the Royal Swazi Sun and business services at the Ezulwini Sun and Lugogo Sun Hotel. Costs are high, and patrons should avoid making telephone calls from this hotel. In the Ilanga Restaurant, both residents and visitors can select from an assortment of meals. Light background music wiles diners into a quiet reverie of tastes, smells and delights. Over weekends, specials are an attraction of the Ilanga, including a family buffet.

Children are a feature of the Lugogo Sun. Most visitors trail at least two additions. To hear children laughing, see their excited faces and be caught up in their young lives is an added attraction of the Lugogo Sun Hotel. You will need to book at least 60 days before arriving. For the Christmas period, make reservations by October at the latest.

Address: Lugogo Sun Hotel, P.O. Box 412, Mbabane, or Private Bag, Ezulwini, Swaziland.

Telephone: (09268) 61101, fax 61111.

Across from the Lugogo Sun Hotel is the comfortable and easy-going Ezulwini Sun.

Ezulwini Sun Hotel: High to medium tariff

With spectacular views to the south-eastern end of the Ezulwini valley, this hotel hosts mainly businessmen. Not as flashy as the Royal Swazi Sun, nor as busy as the Lugogo Sun, the Ezulwini Sun Hotel is quiet, yet with a tension that can only be attributed to the high-level business conferences that are almost a daily event in the conference centre. Business facilities add to the stock market pitch in the business centre. Secretarial services, on-line computers, fax machines and an efficient telephone exchange, make working from the Ezulwini Sun a pleasure.

Although few of the guests notice the setting, the Ezulwini Sun Hotel looks out over the lower areas of Lobamba and up to the rocky summits of the Mdzimba hills. Shops and medical facilities are also available, as is a courtesy bus to the international airport at Matsapha. Guided walks, and horse rides from the Ezulwini Sun Riding Centre, can be arranged, as can packed lunches for guests who want to spend the day exploring the area. Meals can be taken in the hotel dining room from a tasty menu. In addition to the dining room, casual visitors are welcome to arrive, without a booking, for a light lunch or snack at the Coffee Shop.

For relaxation, two tennis courts, a splendid garden, swimming pool and nearby Ezulwini golf driving range are accessible to residents. Visitors can use the pool and tennis facilities by contacting reception. The fee is negligible and the opportunity unexpected. Hitchhikers should consider having an evening meal at the hotel and then retiring to the bar, where they will meet travelling salesmen who can assist in onward travel.

Bookings are necessary.

Address: Ezulwini Sun Hotel, P.O. Box 123, Ezulwini, Swaziland.
Telephone: (09268) 61201, fax 61782.

Leaving the hotel, travel past the riding centre and golf driving range
to the Yen Saan Hotel and Chinese Restaurant.

Yen Saan Hotel and Chinese Restaurant: High tariff

Hidden in an enchanted landscape, this hotel and restaurant takes guests
to China for the length of their visit. Comfort and eastern cuisine are
their specialities. Accommodation is in 34 rooms, all with en suite bathroom, telephone and radio. Should you elect to stay or eat here, make
full use of this voyage to another time and place.

Staff seem a bit bemused by everything and you may need patience
and perseverance to get things done. Still, just enjoying the subtly
scented atmosphere will bring back a flood of memories to those travellers who have experienced the magic of the east. Without a shadow
of doubt, the main attraction at the Yen Saan is its Chinese Restaurant.
It is the best place in the country for authentic oriental food. Vegetarians
are well catered for. An elaborate, diverse menu is available, as are
several daily specialities. Guests are not always informed of the specials,
and you must ask for them. For more active guests, there is tennis and
swimming with dancing on Friday and Saturday nights.

This is an ideal spot at which to stop. Not only is it well situated,
but it will also relax a travel-weary mind to the point where it seems
as though you have stepped into a different country. Tranquillity and
service are the attractions of this unique hotel. Visitors may try arriving
without a reservation at the restaurant, but it is necessary to have made
a prior booking for the hotel.

Address: Yen Saan Hotel and Chinese Restaurant, P.O. Box 771,
             Mbabane, Swaziland.
Telephone: (09268) 61051, fax 61051.

Across the road from the Yen Saan is the 1st Horse Restaurant.

The 1st Horse Restaurant is popular with visitors and offers tasty eastern
and continental cuisine. A varied menu is available, with choices for
vegetarians. Staff are cordial if noncommittal, so do not expect any
recommendations of dishes. This is irrelevant anyway, as no matter
what you choose, it will be good. Reservations must be made at least
12 hours in advance. Tel. 61137.

Leaving the restaurant, follow the road which continues to drop towards the valley floor. The National Handicraft Training Centre (Chinese Handicraft Mission) is a few kilometres down this road. It can be difficult to arrange a visit to one of these handicraft facilities. While welcoming tour groups, the staff seem suspicious of independent travellers. Make an appointment several weeks in advance. If you are successful, the guided walk is both informative and interesting. The blending of African and Chinese culture has resulted in an explosion of colour and craftsmanship.

Address: National Handicraft Training Centre (Chinese Handicraft Mission), Private Bag, Codec Premises, Ezulwini, Swaziland.
Telephone: (09268) 61754.

Follow the billboards to the right, indicating Armstrong Artworks, Mantenga Falls Hotel and Mlilwane Wildlife Sanctuary. This narrow tarred lane winds between thick green vegetation, creating a calming effect after the traffic battles of the main Manzini-Mbabane highway. About 2 km along this road, travellers will notice Smokey Mountain Village on the hillside.

Smokey Mountain Village: Medium tariff

"In the cleavage of Sheba," was the way one Italian guest described Smokey Mountain Village. And indeed, it is the peaks known as Sheba's Breasts that nudge the fringes of these quaint 18 self-catering cottages. Frequented by families and romantic couples, Smokey Mountain Village is close enough to tourist attractions, yet offers wilderness and privacy to residents. Guests are spoiled at Smokey Mountain Village. Without the rush and prices of the big hotels, personal attention is of a high standard. Expect to be treated as VIPs throughout your stay, and do not be surprised if you are back again the following year.

The village is self-catering, but a merry Italian restaurant is also available. The Double-Tot pub will lure many away from their cottages. Built in the manner of an English pub, the same warmth and good humour can be found at the Double-Tot. Families and couples reserve accommodation months ahead, so book at least four to five months in advance.

Address: Smokey Mountain Village, P.O. Box 21, Ezulwini, Swaziland.
Telephone: (09268) 61291, fax 46465.

At Copperland, curio hunters will find an impressive array of copper goods; the intricate copper bangles are cheap, unique and make for wonderful personal jewellery and gifts. Next door is the little Coffee-Time shop where teas and light snacks are on sale throughout the day. Mantenga Crafts beckons most people who have done their homework on Swaziland and is an ethnic shopper's delight. At Mantenga Craft's workshops visitors may watch the crafters at work. Dexterity and creativity appear to be the main criteria at Mantenga and artists are allowed full expression. Finished works are retailed through the Mantenga Foundation. Founded in 1974, the concept of Mantenga Craft Village is based on long-term self-sufficiency.

The choice of completed works is staggering. It would need a whole day to see all the pieces and workshops. But, unlike other tourist shops, there is no rush or pressure on you. Browsing is accepted and occasionally even suggested by assistants. Make a point of going out to the potters studio. Working with one of the first materials ever used by man for art, these potters are skilled, talented and enjoy talking to interested visitors.

You can be certain that your money will be ploughed back into the village and lives of the crafters. This is one place where tourism is beneficial to all.

Entering an area of tall trees, majestic views and natural beauty, travellers pass Mantenga Falls Hotel. The Mantenga Falls are about 3 km of strenuous walking to the south. Do not attempt this walk on your own, crime is high in the area. Instead, wait until getting to the Mlilwane Wildlife Sanctuary from where armed guides can be arranged. This whole district, with its large number of foreign visitors, is prone to a horrendous number of tourist attacks. Strangely, the King lives within sight of this location. The close proximity of his Royal Kraal at Lobamba has done nothing to limit crimes against defenceless visitors. Stay in groups whenever possible or keep to shop and hotel grounds.

Mantenga Falls Hotel: High to medium tariff

Hidden among trees and bush is the Mantenga Falls Hotel. Providing easy access to the local curio shops and art workshops, this hotel is gaining popularity with visitors. The attitude is best described as casual, with an attention to service that is wonderfully refreshing. Accommodation is in 14 double rooms with private washing facilities. Locals throng the pub at night, and although keeping to themselves, enjoy having a foreigner spend time among them. The Mantenga Falls Hotel provides all meals with special arrangements for vegetarian diners. Particularly attractive are the outdoor meals from the Big Tree Restaurant. In the shade of trees and accompanied by bird-song, this is a relaxing place to eat. Reservations are advised for all visitors – whether to the restaurant or accommodation.

Address: Mantenga Falls Hotel, P.O. Box A75, Swazi Plaza, Swaziland.
Telephone: (09268) 61049, fax 61032.

Across the single-lane pontoon bridge, to the south of the hotel, the road becomes gravel. Keep to the right, following the signs for Mlilwane Wildlife Sanctuary and Balnacraig Farm.

Once over the cattle-grid, visitors are within the wildlife sanctuary. The speed limit drops to 25 km/h for obvious reasons. The road continues through old forest and agricultural lands to the entrance of what must rate as Swaziland's most famous and well-managed wildlife refuge.

Mlilwane Wildlife Sanctuary: Medium to low tariff

Draped over hills between the pineapple fields of Malkerns and the populated settlements of the Ezulwini valley is a secret garden called Mlilwane Wildlife Sanctuary. Protected by the rock cliffs of the Mdzimba hills to the north, and the Royal Kraal to the south, Mlilwane marks the founding site of Swaziland's now world renowned wildlife reserves. Established as a conservation area in 1964, Mlilwane pays homage to the perseverance and foresight of two men. The idea, dream and ultimate reality of this wildlife refuge was almost entirely the work of Terence Reilly. Aiding him along every turn, and an active supporter of the cause, was the late King Sobhuza II. Even today, the life of Ted Reilly is inextricably woven into the fabric of Swaziland's nature conservation and propagation programme. Visitors should make every effort to meet this quiet, knowledgable and remarkable man. A recommended purchase for visitors is the attractive book entitled *The Mlilwane Story*. Not only does this fascinating book chart the life and times of the area, it also provides numerous anecdotes, some happy, others sad, but all touched with a unique insight and sensitivity that has all but disappeared in the 20th century.

Flagship of Big Game Parks of Swaziland Holdings, Mlilwane reflects planning, dedication and commitment. While most visitors only spend the day, you should try to stay at least two. Even if you spent a week exploring from the Nyonyane hills, burial site of Swazi royalty to abandoned forests, from Mantenga Falls to tracking down shy and elusive giraffe, you would not see and do everything. Many of the guests have solved the problem by returning repeatedly to Mlilwane. There is a family atmosphere here, a sense of belonging that is encouraged by the well-trained and helpful staff. Despite their fame, the Reilly family still find time to mix with visitors. And now, a Marketing and Tourism manager has been appointed. He continually mingles with guests, giving advice, assistance, and adding to the already legendary hospitality of this famous wildlife sanctuary.

Visitors who are more intent on relaxing and enjoying the serenity of Mlilwane have a number of points at which to lounge about. You may lie around a sparkling swimming pool while sipping a drink and gazing at an incredible view of forests, savanna, hills and distant meadows. Top of the list however, is the hippo pool. Here you will be able to see probably the world's most photographed hippo. Going by the peculiar name of Somersault, this hippo has appeared in magazines, books, brochures and family snaps across the globe. One particular incident of note was when a photo of Somersault was published in a South African travel magazine. This photo had him posing in what was supposed to be a game reserve in Kenya! Some years ago, cereal was put out to encourage birds to nest in the small trees around the pool, but to the ranger's surprise, Somersault decided to also partake. Now, every afternoon he lumbers out of his little lake and eats feed within metres of watchers. This is a major attraction, and the glee on the faces of children and wonder on those of adults speaks volumes for the achievement of wildlife awareness.

Active visitors are also catered for. A favourite is taking part in game viewing on horseback. Experience is not necessary. The horses are gentle and well trained. Horse riding is expensive but the experience and ability to get close to game far outweighs the cost. Graded gravel roads offer a variety of self-drive opportunities. Knowledgeable guides can be hired for these tours. They accompany people in the comfort of their own cars, taking them to spots where they are most likely to see game. If you are unhappy about touring in your vehicle or have arrived by public transport, then book yourself onto one of the open Land Rover excursions, especially the night drive.

Guided hiking trails wind through bush, over hills and alongside streams, taking walkers to the depths of this wildlife wonderland. For solo hikers, the Macobane hill trail offers the chance to commune with nature along an undulating path that rises into the hills above the sanctuary. Walk to the dam. This is the major breeding ground for waterfowl in the kingdom. Plans are under way to buy a locomotive, carriages and a 3,5 km section of railroad that runs through the park. Soon visitors will be able to travel on what will become one of the world's great train rides.

The majority of visitors are locals. They are carefree and jovial, eager to chat and share the untrammelled beauty of the sanctuary. Mlilwane, as a private conservancy, depends entirely on the gate fee that these visitors pay. However, prices are kept low, making it accessible to all who want to experience Swaziland's natural heritage. A large consideration in planning is to include the locals in conservation as much as possible. Sadly, a dark and gory danger also lurks in the bush. Poachers are a continual menace to the rangers and future of Swaziland's wildlife. Backed by foreign investment, armed with automatic weapons, packs of trained hunting dogs and off-road vehicles, they wage a sick and lethal war on many of the rare animal and bird species at Mlilwane. Poaching is a passionate topic at the sanctuary, and if visitors see the destruction and brutality which accompanies this most base of acts, they too will definitely take an anti-poaching stance.

Few people come to Mlilwane to lie in bed all day, but this does not mean that attention to accommodation is lacking. By far the best accomodation is in the seven beehive huts near the forested camp site. The units consist of two huts with three beds, and five huts with two beds. The village has a communal kitchen and spotless ablution facilities. In spartan but comfortable huts, visitors can open themselves to imaginings of tribal life. These huts are very much in demand and reservations need to be made weeks, if not months, in advance. In addition to the huts, there are nine wood and thatch cottages built beneath tall trees within sight of the hippo pool. Eight of these cottages share a fully-supplied communal kitchen and a hot and cold water washing block. The ninth cottage is entirely self-catering and includes four single beds. Under a wild fig tree between the swimming pool and the beehive village is a six roomed, 24 bed dormitory. Camping and caravanning are also encouraged. A secluded forest setting is provided for campers and caravans, as is security for tents.

Although accommodation is classed as self-catering, delicious and affordable meals are available in the Hippo Haunt restaurant which projects over the hippo pool. Beckoning visitors to "Come graze with us," breakfast, lunch and supper are provided. Somewhat short on food for vegetarians, meat-eaters will find a feast by buying a ticket, from the curio, drink and sweet shop, to the campfire grills. Venison is cooked over an open fire, and served with crisp salads. Spoil yourself by eating the venison cooked with tomato and onions. Equally tasty are the hardened maize porridge and fresh vegetables.

Wherever you journey in Swaziland, make a special effort to visit Mlilwane Wildlife Sanctuary. Wildlife abounds with zebra, impala, blue wildebeest, buffalo, warthog, crocodile and of course hippo. You cannot leave Mlilwane without a sense of loss.

Competition for accommodation is fierce so make reservations well in advance to avoid disappointment. If you are unable to get a bed, take along a tent – for which no prior arrangements are necessary.

Address: Mlilwane Wildlife Sanctuary, P.O. Box 33, Mbabane, Swaziland, or Central Reservations, P.O. Box 234, Mbabane, Swaziland.
Telephone: (09268) 45006, fax 61594 or 44246.

Returning to the tarred road, travellers follow the signs for Matsapha and Manzini. Public transport is available in the village of Lobamba. Hitchhiking out of Mlilwane is easy; all you need to do is wait at the main gate. If space is available, most motorists will give you a lift to either the main road or Lobamba.

Prior to continuing with the Ezulwini valley route, pleasure-seeking visitors should return to the main Mbabane-Manzini road. Turn right and look for the Happy Valley Motel.

Happy Valley Motel: High to medium tariff

Aimed unashamedly at entertainment-orientated guests and visitors, this motel has become a legend in Swaziland. It is not a place for families or those in search of peace and silence. There is always a frenzy of activity at the Happy Valley Motel, especially around the swimming pool. Guests are spoiled, pampered, occasionally cuddled, receiving personal attention from motivated, young and vibrant staff. Overnight visitors are provided with accommodation in 57 rooms, equipped with television, two video channels, coffee-making machine, telephone and stocked bar-fridge. Everything has been done to ensure ease for guests. The Happy Valley Motel is a place where everyday cares and worries can be locked up and forgotten in the 24-hour security patrolled parking.

Lunch and supper can be taken in the Sir-Loin steakhouse. Takeaways are available from an equally meaty menu at the Roadhouse. For late-night coffee, very early breakfast or daytime snacks, there is little to beat the Viennese Coffee Shop.

Then there is the notorious and exciting Why Not Disco Night Club. Billed by travel writer Anthony Philpot as "the most decadent place in Swaziland," this is a destination for seekers of loud, debauched night-life, or lunch time strip and cabaret shows. Live bands, loud music and swirling lights are a feast for culture saturated travellers. The last days of Rome could not have been more unrestrained. It is a wonderful place to meet young Swazi people.

Because of the popularity of the Happy Valley Motel, reservations are necessary for accommodation.

Address: Happy Valley Motel, P.O. Box 943, Mbabane, Swaziland. Telephone: (09268) 61061, fax 61050.

Returning to the described route, travel south-east to the royal village of Lobamba. Here, the majestic Ezulwini valley fades into soft rolling hills and disappears into flat, typically African bush.

Painted sky blue, Somhlolo National Stadium is the site for all celebrations of importance in Swaziland. From coronations to music concerts, through international sporting events and pontiffs' visits, the National Stadium is a proud showpiece for the nation.

Annual ritual dances are held in the royal kraal. These can usually only be seen with an official invitation. This is not however so for the colourful and stimulating reed dance, which takes place at the end of August each year. Anyone can view this dance and every effort should be made to arrange your visit to coincide with it. Entrance to the Lozitha Palace is forbidden to those who do not have an official appointment. Security is high. Under all circumstances avoid the temptation to take photographs. This is a vulnerable and high-risk area where misread intentions are guaranteed to either land you beaten and in jail or deported by hardline soldiers as an undesirable alien. If you have time, try and get signed permission to photograph specific things. Photographers should make enquiries telephonically to the Ministry of Information: tel. (09268) 42761 or through the Tourism Ministry: tel. (09268) 42531.

Near Somhlolo Stadium, visitors are able to take a guided tour of the Houses of Parliament. You cannot just turn up and expect to be allowed in. Telephone the offices for current tour starting times: (09268) 61286, fax 61603. There is not a great deal of interest at the parliamentary buildings and most people quickly leave the cold austere passages of power for the attractive National Museum.

The National Museum is next to the Houses of Parliament. Exhibits of early Swazi life to the present day, are informative and lifelike. With the Swazi preference for wearing traditional garb in everyday life, it can often get confusing as to who are the mannequins and whom the humans. Guides are available and will provide in-depth detail on displays. A traditional Swazi village has been constructed outside the museum. Swazi culture and tradition is a puzzle to many Western visitors, but the museum not only offers explanation, it also encourages you to investigate the meanings, legends and myths that make Swaziland the mysterious kingdom that it is. Walking the museum on your own can often be confusing and frustrating. Contact the information office for times and fees of guided tours. The guides' anecdotes, titbits of triviality and astonishing amount of Swazi knowledge, make taking this tour a far cry from glamorous women holding umbrellas above their heads and shouting, "Follow the yellow umbrella."

Address: National Museum, P.O. Box 100, Lobamba, Swaziland. Telephone: (09268) 61151.

Thus ends the Ezulwini valley route. Having enjoyed all the delights that this sliver of Swaziland has to offer, the adventurous will want to proceed beyond the valley – out to the mountains, plains and wide rivers of rural Swaziland.

7 SOUTHERN ROUTE

Lavumisa – Maloma – Sithobela – Kubuta – Grand Valley – Hlatikulu
– Nhlangano – Gege – Sicunusa – Mgazini – Mankayane – Loyengo –
Malkerns
Distance: about 310 km

LAVUMISA

Lying in the south-eastern corner of Swaziland, Lavumisa is one of the
major entry points to the country. There is not a great deal of interest
to visitors. Most people entering Swaziland simply pass through the
border formalities before rushing north to Big Bend, but it can be an
interesting introduction to this region of the country.

Finding your way around this little settlement is very easy. As they
cross the border from South Africa, visitors will find themselves in the
main street. To the right is the bus and minibus taxi depot and behind
that, the Lavumisa Hotel. Few people ever bother staying here, but if
you have time, it is certainly worth the effort. Do not expect five-star
accommodation or even any meals. Instead, consider it an opportunity
to mix with the locals.

Lavumisa Hotel: Medium tariff
Located behind the bus depot, and on a tarred road going east, the
hotel is a step into colonial Swaziland. Unfortunately, what must have
been a gracious and splendid place has now been neglected. Yet, on
moonlit nights when the air is still, it is easy to feel the ghosts of
forgotten guests. Sitting in rattan and cane chairs on the wide veranda
sipping cool drinks, English visitors can be forgiven for becoming
nostalgic.

Now, most of the patrons are locals who make use of the bar, bottle
store and attend occasional dances that take place on Friday and Saturday evenings. If you are not a social person, the bar and disco may
become a little too much for you on weekend evenings.

Accommodation is in double rooms with either shower or bathroom.
Rooms are basic but comfortable. Meals can be something of a problem
– few guests eat at the hotel. Take along your own food for the stay.

MOZAMBIQUE

SOUTH
AFRICA

Swaziland Southern Route

Siteki
Tikuba
Big Bend
Golela
Nsoko
SKILWENI 418
NKONDOLOLO HILLS
Lavumisa
Onverwacht
MKHAYA NATURE RESERVE
Siphofaneni
Sithobela
KALWENE 418
LUGOLWENI HILLS
Sihlutse
Salitje
Helehele
LIBETSE MTS
Ngwane Park
Manzini
Kubuta
Maloma
Mhlosheni
Kwaluseni
Matsapha
SINGENI MTS
Sidvokodvo
Hlatikulu
MHLOSHENI HILLS
Dwaleni
Lobamba
Loyengo
Grand Valley
Nhlangano
Bhunya
Malkerns
Mankayane
Magazini
Lusutfu
MAHLANGATSHA HILLS
MOZAAN KOP 1 171
Mahamba
Sandlane
MBULUNGENI HILLS
Sicunusa
LAPANDA 1 382
HLABENIKOP 1 387
Gege
LAGUBU 1 294
Nerston
Houdkop
Bothashoop

Reservations are not necessary even in peak season. Visitors who prefer having every last detail planned should contact the hotel directly.

Address: Lavumisa Hotel, P.O. Box 54, Lavumisa, Swaziland.
Telephone: (09268) ask for Lavumisa number 7.

Be careful of taking photographs. This is a border area and neither the military nor the RSP (police) appreciate visitors taking photos of places such as the border post, the fence along the border, communication aerials, post office, RSP (police) or railway sidings. Within the settlement, visitors will find fuel at Total Filling Station and Shell Jabula Filling Station. For quick, light snacks, try the grilled chicken from the Big Foot Happy Eater. More filling meals can be found at the Dlanokwakho Restaurant, near the Shell Garage.

The post office and RSP (police) are near one another along the main road. Of interest is the tailor who cuts and stitches away in a car garage. Prices are low and any mending you may have will be done while you wait. The Lavumisa market is small, with a fairly good selection of fruit and vegetables.

Lavumisa is warm and humid, lying in a shallow protected valley less than 100 km from the Indian Ocean. Be prepared for thick vegetation, sweat and happy friendly locals, who readily invite foreigners into their homes as they wander past.

Leaving Lavumisa, proceed north until reaching the route indicators on the edge of town. With a speed limit of 80 km/h, the tarred road continues about 70 km to Big Bend. The trip is not particularly interesting. To follow this described southern route, turn left at the road sign for Hluthi and Nhlangano. Hitchhiking from Lavumisa can be difficult if you are going west. There is not much private traffic along this road. Most people using this route do so by public transport. Five buses per day arrive in and depart from Lavumisa. Of these, only two go west. At 7h00, the first bus leaves and travels to Nhlangano in two hours. At 8h00, the second bus departs for Sithobela. This second ride is long, dusty and crowded. There are stops every 5 km and the trip will take almost six hours. Instead, hitch or take a bus to Nsoko, about 34 km north of Lavumisa. There are several buses throughout the day that leave from Nsoko to Maloma, Sithobela, Kubuta and Hlatikulu.

This road soon becomes gravel, and takes travellers into dense acacia trees and savanna. Traditional mud and thatch villages appear in clearings on either side of the road. Rising into a series of low hills, visitors are afforded clear views of the Lebombo mountains to the east, and nearer, a green and brown patchwork of agricultural lands.

The gravel road gets steadily worse. Low-growing, indigenous thickets of thorn trees edge the road. Behind the trees, barbed-wire fences indicate foreign ownership of the enormous ranches and estates that cover much of south-eastern Swaziland. At Bambanani Women's Association Vegetable Garden and Sales, the road climbs into a jumble of hills. Visitors can buy fresh vegetables at the association's stall. There is always a wide choice, prices are good and you are allowed to select your own items.

Proceeding west, drivers should be alert for stray cattle that wander across the road. For some odd reason they also seem to enjoy lying in the road. Whatever you do, do not kill or crash into cattle. Not only will the damage to your vehicle be extensive, but, as a traveller from Botswana found out, herdboys will soon appear out of the bush. They demand immediate recompense or will get violent and forcibly remove things from the vehicle.

Numerous storks nest in this area and visitors may see them riding the warm thermals in large flocks above the shimmering bush.

West of the small stone quarry is a T-junction. Continue on past the Ndabazezwe High School on the left. Camping is permitted at the school. There are however no facilities. It is better to seek accommodation further west at the Phaphamani Mswati Store. Set in hills bedecked with aloes, there is a school located behind the store. The teachers here are delighted to meet visitors. You will be given a tour of the school, and asked to listen to recitals in Swazi and English. It is a fascinating and humbling experience. Accommodation can be arranged by speaking to the principal.

Habitation decreases west of the school and store. This is definitely not a common tourist route. The road climbs steeply over hills. In the wet season drivers should be prepared for lots of sliding about and poor traction. Wildflowers abound along this section. Stretching up hillsides, they create colourful patterns against the green of the trees. Birds make a cacophony of sounds, scents from flowers and soil touch the senses and the enormous sky quietens the soul. The Mhlosheni hills to the west shield distant Nhlangano, while to the north low hills indicate that, should you proceed north, you will enter the valleys of the Ngwavuma and Mhlathuze rivers.

Small intensively cultivated family plots become frequent. Milk and vegetables can occasionally be bought from these kraals. On Saturday and Sunday you will be expected to stay for at least one drink of cereal beer. Take care. Cereal beer is unlike any ordinary beer and its effects are far more intoxicating. In the humidity and heat of the region you may soon find yourself resting under some tree in the kraal, the rest of the day forgotten in a euphoric haze of tribal Swaziland.

Plots are cultivated with the aid of donkeys pulling heavy mould-board ploughs. It is excruciating work for the ploughman, and the stubbornness of the donkeys means that plots larger than one acre cannot be finished in a day.

Matsanjeni Health Centre is new, efficient, and harsh on the eyes as it suddenly appears out of the bush. Surrounded by a fence, it undertakes a vital responsibility in the area. Both the health centre and neighbouring Ebuhleni Grocery shop are frequently lashed by violent storms. The results can be seen in the buckled roofs, washaways and broken trees. From the health centre west, the bush has been hacked back to make place for maize, cotton and bean fields. Cotton is the main crop grown, and while maize is the staple food, cotton is the revenue earner. An easy relaxed pace infects the area. The scenes of people hoeing under wide-brimmed hats, feeding babies or resting, is reminiscent of Giorgione's paintings.

Erosion is reaping its own deadly harvest from the monoculture system practised. Serious reclamation programmes will need to be carried out if local agriculture is to survive.

Bus drivers reach high speeds down these hills, hoping to gather momentum to climb the next rise. Other vehicles are advised to get well to the edge of the road when they see one of these buses approaching.

Local streams are used for all manner of things. Over weekends, buses, cars and minibus taxis are washed and mopped down. Mondays and Thursdays women bring their laundry down for a pounding. Throughout the week livestock drink, youths fish hopefully and children splash about in merriment. Ask before taking photographs of these activities. The reputation that many visitors have of being exploitive should always be borne in mind.

With the road becoming an assault course, you will pass the Matilankhatsa Supermarket and then arrive at Matsanjeni Restaurant, where BP fuel is available.

Not only is there excellent traditional food available, but visitors can also ask for accommodation, which will be found in local villages.

Diners and drinkers at the restaurant are reserved and suspicious at first. But, once they realise that you are just a visitor, here to see their magnificent country, you will be adopted for your stay. There is wonderful hiking country near the Sitilo river. Old trails lead through dense bush and onto the summits of tall hills. Particularly good views can be found near the sign for Mageyidini Station (about 24 km from Lavumisa.) Walk or drive along the edge of the cotton field to the small kraal at the foot of the steep hill. The old headman will gladly allow you to not only walk to the summit, but also camp up there. A basic meal can be negotiated at the kraal, and you will be invited to eat with the family. It is enchanting watching the faces of children and adults as the firelight flickers in the fragrant night breeze.

Contoured lands fill most of the valleys around Mageyidini. The wilderness further east is replaced by the orderliness of rows of cotton. Travellers may find themselves hurrying west, in the hope of regaining nature's playground. Across the single-lane bridge visitors will encounter a sign indicating straight on for Nhlangano and Hluthi, left to Salitje border post and on to Pongola in South Africa and right towards Maloma and Manzini. This crossroad is about 32 km from Lavumisa. Visitors following the southern route turn right here.

The gravel road cuts through aloe and acacia covered hills. Alongside the road, there is a proliferation of huts and human habitation. You will be expected to share the road with untended livestock. A small causeway, which floods in the wet season, takes travellers back into maize and cotton fields.

Next to the Emphelandzaba Clinic (Makhava Rural Clinic) is the Makhava Market and Handicrafts. The market has a limited supply of goods, while the handicrafts are located in the B.B. Beauty Salon. Dresses, scarves, grasswork and a few statuettes are highly priced and not from Shiselweni province. Clustered around the market is the A1 Store and Shell fuel station.

Continuing north, the road skirts Sibani Vegetable Gardens on the left. You are welcome to buy at the gardens, and pick produce yourself. Leaving the gardens, visitors descend to the concrete causeway over the wide, sluggish Ngwavuma river. This shallow brown river eventually spills into the mighty Phongolo river in South Africa, to the east. There is the most disastrous erosion taking place along the banks of the river. As you drop towards the river from the south, stop and look at the plunging gulleys and virtual canyons that have resulted from floods, droughts and poor veld management. Down at water level, cool breezes ruffle the water and cool travellers. Bilharzia is endemic to rivers in this region and visitors should avoid the temptation to swim.

Proceeding north from the river, the road climbs steeply through a corridor of naboom and acacia trees. As the road improves you can clearly see the varied soil types of this area. The colours of the road surface change from brown to red to orange to pink and back to brown. Barbed wire is replaced by natural barriers of thorn tree branches. Kraals become spiny fortresses behind which cattle, goats and children are kept at night. Unlike the rest of Swaziland, visitors will see men, armed with old bolt-action rifles, along this section. This is a harsh region of natural violence.

Sigwe is marked by a bus stop, fruit and vegetable market, post office and further out, a community of beehive huts near the Nxulu Community Dam and Garden. Malangeni Bus Transport services this area. Their buses are fast, cheap, always crowded but seldom regular. From Elulakeni Secondary School there are stupendous panoramas across the flatness of eastern Swaziland to the Lebombos. Few signs of modernisation are evident in these hills. Men and youths carrying traditional weapons are commonplace.

The President Supermarket is a surprise in the bush. It is modern, clean and well stocked. Fresh bread, fruit and vegetables, perishables and groceries can all be found here. After the basic supplies of other stores on the route from Lavumisa, this is a virtual shopping centre.

Behind Nigunjane Grocery is a small dam where you may camp. Ask at the shop for directions to the local chief to obtain permission. He is an amiable old man who speaks good English and has enough stories to last most of the night. No-one expects any payment for camping at the dam, but some form of appreciation in the form of clothing or food is always welcome. From the dam, the road continues through the Swazi bush to the T-junction village of Maloma.

Only a handful of visitors ever stop in **Maloma.** Those who do usually only get fuel from the BP Filling Station. A large green and white sign gives the directions to other points in Swaziland. Straight to Sithobela, right for Big Bend and Nsoko. Many buses congregate in Maloma outside the Maloma Central Store. A small, but good, market serves the local community and public transport passengers.

Departing along the southern route, follow the sign for Sithobela and travel past the Caltex Farmers Service onto a washboard gravel road. The lands on either side of the road are once again fenced in behind strands of barbed wire. From Nkonjwa Clinic, roadside habitation disappears. Only in the distance, on hillsides and in bush clearings, can huts be seen. This is ranching country, a country of sleek healthy Nguni crossbred cattle and well-managed veld. Past the signs showing the way to Sithobela, Maloma and St Philips, is the entrance to the renowned Mhlatuze Breeding Ranch. A unique blend of African and imported practices is being used at the breeding ranch. Swaziland prides herself on the excellent Nguni cattle that are bred in the country.

North of the ranch, the road crosses the Mhlatuze river, passes Madvubeni General Dealer – where tasty chicken stew can be bought with finely milled hot porridge and a tangy sauce – and enters a thoroughly tribal region. Kraals with beehive or mud huts shelter beneath trees. Men wear traditional maroon and beige skirts and carry sticks, spears and shields. Women go topless in black skirts and beautiful hairstyles. Children run around naked and foreign visitors are totally unexpected. You are certain of a welcome if you stop at any of the kraals.

Maize is grown intensively on strips of flat land. Each plot is jealously protected by thorn-branch walls from the covetous eyes of roaming cattle. Numerous knob thorn trees (*Acacia nigrescens oliv.*) can be found along the sides of the road. These knobbly trees are indications of sweetveld grazing in the area.

Further on, at Nkonjwa Secondary School, campers may find a pitch at either the school or the adjacent modern clinic. Camp in the clinic grounds if possible. It is more comfortable there – provided you can wheedle permission out of the administrator. If you have to, try the school. It is exposed and, apart from a cold-water tap, there are no facilities.

Once past the school, visitors arrive at the tiny settlement of Sithobela, and encounter a road sign pointing the way left to Kubuta and Hlatikulu and right to Siphofaneni. Mpompota Wholesalers has an interesting collection of goods for sale. These range from plastic shoes and ghetto-blasters to groceries and building materials. There is always a crowd in the shop as it supplies most of the area with hardware materials. A government cattle-dipping yard dominates the scene. Every Thursday, during summer, there is a melée of cattle, people and splashing water.

Turn left, taking the gravel road for Kubuta which is about 14 km further west. A well-supplied market is located on the left of the road. There is an abundance of sub-tropical fruit, plus other varieties, and a bewildering selection of crisp, reasonably priced vegetables. Prices are not fixed and bargaining is expected. Try not to disappoint them in this regard. With most buyers being from local villages and kraals, it is something of an event when a visitor stops to purchase. The litchis, mangoes and bananas are especially delicious.

From the street market, the road enters the green hills around the Sibowe river. Vegetation is thick and the climate hot and incredibly humid for a district so far inland. Near a little stone-walled church is another of the community projects, Litsemba Labomake Vegetable Garden.

Large traditional villages are found in these valleys, but the people are not friendly and the children run away screaming when they see a white person. In discussions with some of the locals, I could get no real answer to this strange behaviour. Some said it had to do with an old white family who still farmed in the area. Others claimed fear of South African attitudes. Nothing definite could be found and the people remained distant and suspicious.

Across the Mphophatsa river, the road passes a small trading store, where fuel is available, followed by a slight rise to **Kubuta.** The settlement is reached by taking the left turn, off the main gravel road. This is a terrible road and shows signs of obvious neglect.

Kubuta is a typical African backwater settlement. While a chief supposedly controls the area, it is the descendants of the family Pierce, and later Wales, who dominate the land and provide most employment.

There is not much to Kubuta, but for hikers it is the ideal place from which to start a hike into the mountains to the south-west. A small post office is to the left, as you climb the donga-filled road past the old estate house. The postmaster is a cordial tribal man who arrives for work dressed in long-sleeved shirt, tie, thick jacket and cowhide skirt. In the settlement is a circle and the main buildings of Kubuta: Kubuta Store, BP fuel bowsers and a busy bus stop. Regular buses can be taken from Kubuta to most of the district and to Hlatikulu, Sithobela, Siphofaneni and Maloma. There is a schedule, but it is ignored by the drivers who wait until their vehicle has enough passengers. Hitchhiking is difficult during the week, but easy over weekends when traffic travels to and from Hlatikulu.

Walkers should ask to leave their car at Kubuta Store. From here, take the gravel road that winds past the dip towards the villages scattered across the mountains. This road becomes a path and turns south, over the spurs of steep hills. Follow this path past the large huts in the saddle of the mountain, then turn south-east for the summit. Awesome views extend in all directions. It is a lonely, quiet place, inhabited only by shy herdboys, grazing cattle and browsing goats.

Turn left out of Kubuta, back onto the main road running west. Continue past the colourful sign indicating the entrance to the Kubuta Banana Estates. Between the Memitsi and Batane rivers, visitors should park their vehicle if they want to walk south-west into the thick bush.

Rounded hills and deep valleys drop away as the road climbs to Ngobolweni Community Water Supply. From here, the drive is made along a road that takes travellers to the banks of the Sibhowe river. With wide sandy banks, the river is popular with local youngsters and crowded with cattle. Both regard with curiosity those who stop. Cows sniff you, children laugh and the experience can be unique for city dwellers. Many of the rivers in these hills contain crocodiles and it is inadvisable to go swimming without first thoroughly checking the banks and deep pools.

Rising sharply from the river, the road crosses a range of green hills. There are numerous villages along the way. Stop at any of these and ask to buy some wild honey. Rich, creamy and sweet, the thick wedges of comb are a delight to visitors who have a sweet tooth. At some of these villages fresh fruit can be bought. In season (late December, early January), bunches of enormous juicy litchis can be found on sale.

About 8 km from Kubuta there is a turn-off north. It is possible to continue along the main road directly to Hlatikulu, approximately 15 km to the south-west. But, for a real sight of rural Swaziland, turn right at this turn-off. It is driveable in the summer months by all vehicles, though cycling could be a problem once into the hills. Only one bus per day travels this district road between Sidvokodvo and Hlatikulu. It reaches the turn-off from Hlatikulu at about 7h00. The ride takes approximately two and a half hours to Sidvokodvo. The same bus returns, leaving Sidvokodvo at around 13h00. Hitchhiking is almost impossible along this road as not more than a handful of vehicles pass along it. If you have the stamina, begin walking. It is a pleasant walk, except in the rain. Vehicles that do pass nearly always stop.

This is a good gravel road. Trees become more sparse and grasslands wave from surrounding hills. Deep valleys are split by small streams. Infrequently, a kraal will be seen far from the road. From the entrance to Sisa Ranch, habitation disappears and cattle roam among the trees and tall grass.

Finally, you will arrive at the entrance to Lhiko Letekulima Cattle Breeding Station. Set in a deep wooded ravine, this breeding station is a model of animal and wilderness management. Each programme is carefully monitored and collated, with results being made available to farmers throughout Swaziland.

Further north from the breeding station, visitors follow the course of a small tributary of the Sibowe river. First, down alongside the stream through a mixture of willow and acacia trees, then up, 20 m above it. Road warning signs indicate slippery roads. This is especially true when it rains. Washaways are a common sight on the steeper hills, and boulders in the road can be expected. The road continues through old abandoned contour lands, into the valley which houses the RSP (police) at Ka-Phunga.

A few hundred metres north-west of the sign to Moti Station is a Y-junction. The right hand branch is a gravel road for about 9 km before it joins up with the tarred road north to Sidvokodvo. Keep left, as far as the T-junction with the Grand Valley road that lies between Manzini to the north and Nhlangano to the south. Hitchhikers will find getting rides becomes a great deal easier. Traffic is frequent between the two major urban centres. Buses and minibus taxis speed from north to south and back again throughout the day. Just flag them down in the direction you wish to go. Public transport however does not travel through Grand Valley after about 18h30 or before 7h00.

The southern route doubles back here and goes south-south-west towards Nhlangano. Turn left, south of the bridge over the Mkhondvo river. The road runs parallel to the river as it flows through one of Swaziland's most beautiful areas, **Grand Valley.** With high tree-covered hills standing as natural sentries to the west and east, the Lusutfu river to the north, and Hlatikulu to the south, Grand Valley was a secret known only to the Swazis until the late 1800s.

Vertical cliffs poke their heads out above the slopes. Rock climbing in Swaziland does not have a large following and many of these cliffs are still unclimbed – a challenge if you have the right equipment.

Roadside stalls occur frequently along the route. Roasted corn on the cob and hot creamy porridge are a favourite with the minibus taxi drivers. Any hungry traveller would do well to buy a meal here. They are unusual and filling.

As the road commences a gentle climb, strange and unexplained erosion marks striate the cliffs. No-one in the area seems to know how long they have been there or what caused them. Visitors keen on hiking should consider this region in their plans. Less than an hours drive from the bustling urban centre at Nhlangano, it is possible to cover a large part of the district and return to town before evening. If arriving with your own transport, leave the vehicle parked at the Ekuphumleni Primary School. Should school be in session, get permission from the headmaster.

Dry riverbeds, which occur sporadically, are something of a phenomenon. Water flows along hundreds of streams and many rivers through Grand Valley, yet between the full courses, dry riverbeds lie empty. The most logical explanation, according to geography teacher Mandla Mgaga – who teaches at the local school – is that due to the violent storms which regularly occur, the watercourses are altered by the ferocity of the flow.

Every available patch of flat land is intensively cultivated; maize, vegetables and sorghum are tended in neat, grey-earthen gardens. The sluggish Mkhondvo river flows near the road at this point. A foreign-funded suspension bridge traverses the river. Made of wood, wire and stone, crossing over it is an experience.

Mawelawela Grocery store is a good place from which to start a short hike. The proprietor will let you park behind the store and assign a child to guard your vehicle. Stupendous views can be had by following the ridge up to the right of the store. It is a difficult hike of about one hour to the summit. The heat and humidity can make the walk arduous, but the rewarding view is definitely worth the effort. Buy some fresh fruit at Mawelawela before setting off. A guide can be arranged but is not necessary; there are well-trodden paths up the hill.

Finally, the road reaches the start of the ascent out of Grand Valley. A signboard shows the way to Hlatikulu, Nhlangano and Mahamba.

South of the Sita Sive grocery the tarred road splits into two carriageways. The right hand one is lower and steeper; the left, higher and more gentle. Where the roads rejoin, pull off and look back the way you have come. Almost all the way to Sidvokodvo, the Grand Valley lies below you. It is usually veiled in a heat haze with a soft fragrant breeze spilling up over the hills. Another route indicator points the way either straight to Mahamba, or left to Hlatikulu. Stay on the Mahamba road. Hitchhikers or those using public transport will find most rides going directly to Nhlangano, thereby missing out Hlatikulu. Hlatikulu is less than 10 km from the main road and worth the detour.

This description includes the settlement of Hlatikulu so turn left at this point.

Shortly after turning for Hlatikulu, beyond Salema Grocery store, is a route sign indicating left to Mbulungwane and Kubuta and right to Hlatikulu.

HLATIKULU

Kipling wrote fondly of hill stations in India. These were colonial holiday resorts in the cool hills, where the upper-class British went to escape the blistering heat of the Deccan in summer. Hlatikulu has all the characteristics of a hill station. Mist is common, as are days of cool light drizzle. After travelling through the dust and heat of the flat plains and the humidity of deep valleys, it is sheer bliss to arrive in Hlatikulu.

The entrance to the town from the north is marked by a noticeable increase in the number and height of trees, with tall communication antennae, giraffe-like, behind them. There is a single main road through town. Lying in a north-south grid, Hlatikulu is quiet, cool and welcoming.

Assegai Inn: Medium tariff

The Assegai Inn is opposite the Transtate Bus Service depot. It is cheap, with clean, spacious double and single rooms. Few foreigners ever stay at the Assegai Inn and even fewer tourists.

Do not expect a great deal in your room – after all, it is only for sleeping in. Washing facilities are available both on an individual basis and communally. The bar at the Inn is the focal point over weekends. The crowd is friendly, heavy drinking and talkative. If you are alone, it will only be a matter of minutes before someone joins you (if more than one, you will be left alone).

There does not seem to be any fixed closing time at the bar, and by the time the last singing customer has tumbled out of the door, dawn is only a few hours away.

Reservations can be made, and must be confirmed seven days before arrival.

Address: Assegai Inn, Prince Arthur St, Hlatikulu, Swaziland.
Telephone: (09268) 76126.

Fuel is available at both BP and Engen filling stations in town. At Hlatikulu Public Health, emergency medical treatment is available.

Treatment is free but a donation is recommended. Give it to the reception clerk on leaving. Groceries and hardware can be purchased at the Lucky 7 Supermarket which is near the post office. The postal service at Hlatikulu is quick and efficient. Telephone calls out of the country can be made directly from the public telephone booth outside the post office. If you have any problems, speak to the postmaster, who will allow you use of his office to make the call.

Turning east at the post office, a gravel road leads down to the Tumble Inn and public transport depot. Buses and minibus taxis line up for passengers here. Street vendors and hawkers crowd the perimeter of the square Sahara-like ground. You can buy cooked food, handicrafts, clothing and live chickens from these people. By evening they are no longer the rich brown colour of the Swazi but a pale orange, from all the dust kicked up by buses and taxis.

Trees line the side streets of Hlatikulu and the air is tinged with the scent of conifer and gum. The Tumble Inn does not actually signify accommodation – though it can be arranged via the bartender. Its name is deceiving however, and if you spend any length of time in the bar, you will see that the opposite is true: walk in, tumble out. It is a good place to get information on buses, taxis and routes. The drivers can often arrange a special fare for travellers. Buses for Nhlangano arrive and depart from about 5h30 to 19h00. Taxis run to their own schedule, depending on how many passengers they can squash into their vehicles before leaving.

Back at the post office, visitors will notice the VIP Dry-Cleaners across the road. Same day laundry can be done here. Get the washing in early and at around midday it can be collected clean and ironed. Prices are low and service excellent. At the Shishelweni Tea Room, good American-style takeaways are available. Pims Restaurant and Bar near the southern extremity of town has a basic menu of mainly traditional food.

To leave Hlatikulu and return to the main Nhlangano road, turn right (i.e. west) at the post office. Take the turning for Nhlangano and Mahamba past Lusoti Traders through groves of blue gum trees. At the T-junction, turn left for Mahamba and Nhlangano and right to Sidvokodvo and Manzini. Basic motor repairs can be done at Harris Motor Repairs. It may be difficult to see at first; look for the Midway Filling Station and Store which is alongside.

Rising from the filling station, the road enters an area of tall forests, steep valleys and the domain of Shiselweni Forestry Company.

Shiselweni mill is cocooned in a blanket of eucalyptus scent. Tours of the forests and mill can be arranged, but prior booking is essential. Contact the head office at Emfomfeni.

Address: Shiselweni Forestry Company, P.O. Box 98, Nhlangano, Swaziland.
Telephone: (09268) 78411, fax 78713.

Between the patches of hillside, where there is no planted forest, houses, huts and kraals claim the soil for small subsistence plots. This continues until the turn-off to the Embangweni military barracks. Photographs are forbidden within a radius of 5 km and visitors are advised to obey this instruction. Houses become more modern, built with bricks and with tile roofs. Around Nsongweni High School, lantana weed competes in size with forest trees. Lantana and guava trees are Swaziland's worst exotic invaders. In the game reserves, a never-ending war against guava and lantana has led to the formation of eradication programmes using local labour.

This region is full of natural splendour and wonderful walking country. High meadows carpeted in thick green grass and wildflowers, tumbling streams and silent forests abound.

A large "Welcome to Nhlangano" sign is placed about 100 m from the T-junction. Turn left and continue on the tarred road past the Agricultural Research station. At the second junction, the road either goes straight on to the Nhlangano Sun Hotel and Casino, or turns, at right angles, into the town of Nhlangano.

NHLANGANO

Meaning "Meeting Place," Nhlangano is the southern agricultural centre for timber, maize and small quantities of tobacco. Queen Elizabeth II visited this urban settlement in 1947 with her father King George, to meet with Swaziland's King Sobhuza II. Local legend says that is why the name was changed from Goedgegun to Nhlangano shortly after the historic meeting.

Upon entering Nhlangano from the north-east, visitors pass the stadium on the left. Regular sporting events take place here, notably football matches on Saturday and Sunday afternoons. Details can be obtained by contacting the RSP (police) in town. The Evelyn Baring High School nestles in a wooded garden before the town's suburbs. During school vacation, visitors with their own tents may be allowed to camp in the grounds, with access to washing facilities. Prior arrangements have to be made at least two months in advance. Write to: Evelyn Baring High School, P.O. Nhlangano, Nhlangano, Swaziland, tel. (09268) 78210.

Emantimandze Butchery offers roasts with free porridge. Its motto, "We feed the nation," is a direct reflection on the entrepreneurial skills of the owner.

Superparts Spares has a range of new and used spares for motorists. Negotiation of prices is expected for both new and old parts. Nearby is the Phoenix Hotel.

Phoenix Hotel: Medium tariff

On the north-eastern side of town, the Phoenix Hotel is a good place to meet people. Accommodation is in double and single rooms. Groups of up to four are allowed to sleep in the double rooms. Ablution facilities are provided, but travellers are advised to wear plastic sandals while washing. Cleanliness does not rate too highly at this establishment, whose main source of income is from alcohol sales. Meals are provided from a verbal menu, with breakfast included in the accommodation tariff. Vegetarians are in for a hungry stay. It might be a good idea to purchase some fruit and vegetables at the market if you intend staying here. The cook will gladly prepare the vegetables at no extra cost. If you are to eat breakfast, place the order before going to sleep.

Dingy and empty during the week, over weekends the Phoenix Hotel erupts into a vibrant, loud and thoroughly enjoyable gathering place for locals.

Hotel reservations are not necessary, but visitors should note that the reception desk is closed from about 20h00, after which you will have to track down the manager at home.

Address: Phoenix Hotel, P.O. Box 360, Nhlangano, Swaziland. Telephone: (09268) 78488.

Further into Nhlangano, visitors will find a BP fuel station, Webster's Bookshop (where daily international and Swazi newspapers can be bought), and the regional headquarters of the RSP (police). Hungry Jacks sells a good selection of light meals at reasonable prices. It takes time for them to fill the order so place your order then wander around town for about 15 minutes. Past the Shell filling station is a branch of Barclay's Bank. For foreigners, this bank is arguably the most efficient in Swaziland. Daily, they are required to change foreign currency, cash travellers cheques and issue cash against credit cards. Their facilities are modern and fast. It should take no longer than five to ten minutes to complete a financial transaction. On Saturdays you should get there by at least 8h45 to avoid having to spend hours in long queues. Next door is Swaziland Development and Savings Bank. Not a touch on Barclay's, trying to do foreign exchanges is tedious and frustrating. Clerks are not comfortable with international transactions, and a few even admit to sending visitors to Barclay's Bank. Standard Chartered Bank is also fairly good. Their handling charges are high and become ridiculous if a credit card is used. Transmission of money from abroad is possible and takes about two to three days before you are allowed to withdraw. Very popular with locals, there is often a lot of waiting. If however you bank with Standard Bank in your home country, you are likely to get preferential treatment as well as a cup of tea while your money is being cleared.

At the southern end of town is a T-junction in front of the Nhlangano Mall. There is little of interest to the left. The road passes the Swaziland Tobacco Company and Shell garage. To the right, the road skirts the Mall and loops back around the western side of this busy agricultural town. It is straight, towards the Mall, that visitors should go.

Park your vehicle at the RSP (police) near the Phoenix Hotel. They will look after it while you wander about town. Motorcyclists and cyclists should request that their packs be stored in a lock-up room. Backpackers can leave their packs at the RSP (police) as well – you may be asked to open it up for an inspection first.

The Nhlangano Mall is a vibrant mixture of Swazi, Oriental and European influences. Inside the mall, modern shops stock the latest fashions and vacuum sealed supermarket foods. Around the outside of the mall, in countless narrow stalls and shops, you will be able to find virtually everything: tailors, cobblers, barbers, welders, motor spares and so on, including people surreptitiously offering the latest cameras, firearms or drugs. Tourists rave about the markets and bazaars of North Africa, Asia and India, but here, in the hills of southern Swaziland, must surely be one of the best.

To the west of the mall is the Nhlangano bus and taxi depot. Here too, is a multitude of informal sector selling. Food is the main item on sale, including grilled chicken, porridge, potatoes with a fiery sauce, freshly baked bread, fresh fruit and vegetables. Both quality and quantity are good. A meal of hard porridge and chicken pieces wrapped in paper provides ideal travelling food for long bus trips.

More than 20 buses can be found at the depot on any morning. Taxis are fewer but in greater demand due to their higher travelling speeds. Finding transport out of Nhlangano is seldom a problem. Buses travel in all directions from the town. North to Manzini and all villages in between, east through Hluthi to Lavumisa, and west turning south-west, for Mahamba border, or further west towards Gege and beyond. Most of the transport goes north. Two per day go to Lavumisa, two per day towards Gege and at least five per day to Mahamba. Make certain to get there early as the buses and taxis fill up quickly.

A walk around the loop, west of the mall, will take you into the light industrial side of town. Wide roads, trucks, fumes, grease and motor parts are the characteristics of this part of town. It is hectic but worth a tour.

To reach the Nhlangano Sun Hotel and Casino, return north-east out of town to the T-junction.

Nhlangano Sun Hotel and Casino: High tariff

Temple to the god Mammon, the Nhlangano Sun Hotel and Casino once flourished, with a continuous stream of visitors from gambling-starved South Africa. Recently however, a loosening of regulations in that country has allowed gaming establishments to open their doors. The number of guests arriving to gamble at the Nhlangano Casino has correspondingly crashed. To make up for the loss of revenue, hotel and casino prices have jumped. They are now almost beyond the pocket of most average visitors, and even meals will be found expensive.

Perched above the attractive Makhosini valley, the hotel was once regarded as having the most efficient and personalised service in the kingdom. Sadly, that is no longer true. Staff in the Makhosini Restaurant are often rude and impatient, noticeably with disabled guests. Still, there is a great deal to do for the energetic resident. Horse riding and golf are easily arranged: golf on a nine-hole course at the nearby country club, and horse riding from a local stable. A large clean pool is available on the grounds, as are two all-weather tennis courts. Cinemas showing x-rated movies used to be popular with visitors from harshly censored South Africa, but that too, has now changed. Two Kings bar is a popular watering hole.

Accommodation is provided in 48 picturesque chalets. Spacious, lavishly furnished and airconditioned, the charming rooms all have private bathrooms, impressive views, telephone, television and private terrace. Luring the visitor who wants relaxation may have to become the main marketing strategy for the hotel. At night a dramatic Jekyll and Hyde change occurs. The 777 Disco, casino and à la carte restaurants come alive. Dress at the gaming tables is formal, as is the tone. At the computerised games, casual wear is acceptable. Glass, neon, mirrors and flashing lights put the disco anywhere in the world. Drinks are very expensive, prostitutes are a nuisance and it closes early in comparison to other nightclubs. Reservations are required for the hotel though you are just as likely to get a room if you turn up unannounced.

Address: Nhlangano Sun Hotel and Casino, Private Bag Nhlangano,
             Nhlangano, Swaziland.
Telephone: (09268) 78211, fax 78402.

Back at the T-junction, out of Nhlangano, there is a signboard indicating the way right to Mhlosheni. It was to the fertile hills and valleys between Dwaleni and Mhlosheni that Ngwane I led the forefathers of the modern Swazi. In a now forgotten kraal outside Mhlosheni, he died in 1780, father of the Swazi nation. The area is obviously rich in historical Swazi facts, but research is nonexistent. Walkers are free to go wandering about the hills between these two tiny settlements. As well as spectacular views, thick bush, rivers and traditional villages, you will be able to meet possibly the purest bloodlines of the Swazi. There is a sense of history in the old kraals. Even white-haired elders cannot remember when many of them were first built. Legends and myths will beguile those foreigners who stay at some of the more remote villages east of Zombodze. Foreigners are uncommon in these valleys, but the happy, hospitable Swazis will welcome you.

When you continue with the southern route, travel back past the entrance to Nhlangano town and go further west to the T-junction with the road from Manzini. Take the left turn, as indicated by the sign to Mahamba. This is a good place from which to hitchhike north or west. Traffic is heavy along this road and while some motorcar drivers will request payment, the lorry drivers are delighted to have company for a while. Travel past the Fire Station with its drill tower, bright yellow water tenders, pumps and emergency rescue vehicles. West of the timber yard, about 4 km from Nhlangano, there is a turn-off from the main road. To reach the South African border at Mahamba stay on the tarred road for about another 12 km.

Rather than go out of Swaziland, take the turning to Gege. This sign is alongside the enormous advertisement for Sappi Novobord. A good gravel road plunges into exotic forest plantations. Little public transport uses this road, and if you miss the bus or cannot flag down a taxi, start hitchhiking. It may take several lifts before reaching your destination, as there is also not much private traffic. The advantages of hitchhiking this route are that most traffic will stop, and they drive at amazing speeds.

Most of the trees are wattle, gum and conifers. Their scents and silence produce a pleasant tranquillity as you travel up and down low hills to the Sappi Novobord factory. As expected, noise, pollution and dirt are everywhere. Strict security is enforced, and as well as not being allowed to take photographs, uninvited visitors are not welcome. It does not really have anything to interest most visitors anyway. West of the factory, the forests are replaced by rolling grasslands, before dropping to hundreds of hectares of agricultural land, planted with maize in summer.

Jabula Store is the site for the local bus stop. There is an interval of four to six hours between buses passing this way. Across the bridge over the Mkhondvo river, forests take over again. Planted to the edge of the gravel road, they create a cool, green world of shadows and picnic spots.

In the side valleys, gulleys with waterfalls ending in deep pools offer cool swims. A profusion of birdlife can be found in the indigenous woodlands around these pools. Planted forests resume all the way to the RSP's (police) Gege station which stands among lofty exotics. In the tiny settlement of Gege, visitors will come to a signboard in the middle of the village: right to Mbabane and Sicunusa, straight for Piet Retief and the border post with South Africa at Bothashoop.

Camping is permitted in the grounds of the Eric Rosenberg Secondary school. Water and simple washing facilities will be provided. During school time, expect a lot of conversation with the pupils and staff.

Turning right, along the Mbabane/Sicunusa gravel road, you pass the Zamani Grocery. Fresh bread is available, as is milk and a few tinned supplies.

North of the grocery the road meanders across a table-flat landscape. The Gege Maize Project is worth a visit during the harvest in late summer, early autumn. Using local labour and machinery, the fields become a hive of activity. It can get very dusty, but this, combined with the searing heat, makes for some spectacular photography. Past the agricultural lands, strange pebble-strewn hills give the scene a decidedly Scottish moor appearance – particularly when mist descends on wet days. Make a point of climbing to the summit of one of these hills.

Breathtaking panoramas open in all directions. It takes about two hours of moderately difficult walking to reach the summit of the hill that parallels the road. The magnificence all around is inspiring.

At the large dairy farm, visitors can buy fresh warm milk if you have a container. The management are friendly and are willing to allow visitors to pitch a tent near the farm buildings.

Across the single-lane bridge over the Ndlozane river, travellers pass through brightly painted settlements huddled beneath wattle trees. A large sign points the way right, to Mahlangatsha Rural Development Area, about 12 km away. Continue straight on into an area of cultivated contours and terraces.

In a series of wide sweeping bends the gravel road climbs to Sicunusa. Shell fuel is available at Sicunusa Store. Travellers can reach the Sicunusa/Houdkop border by continuing straight on. The border is about 5 km away and is seldom busy. This means that almost no public transport makes the trip there. A minibus taxi can be taken but unless you are the last passenger, you are in for a long wait. Hitchhiking will prove far more fruitful and time saving.

Turn right at the sign which shows the way to Mankayane, Mbabane and Manzini. Marked as the M4, it immediately enters thick forests. Wattle and mimosa line the road; in summer their flowers are a visual delight, their fragrance captivating.

At Mgazini there is a small store that sells BP fuel. There is no real reason for stopping in Mgazini unless you are a hiker. To the west, the fringes of the great Usutu forests can be seen. North-east of the store and filling station, the road runs across a summit ridge with views to the midland valleys of central Swaziland and the highland hills of the western border. From the summit, travellers drop into wide valleys that are heavily populated and intensively cultivated. The tribal heritage is almost nonexistent in this region, with modern houses and no traditional attire or ancient religious practices. Next to the Thuthuka Cash Store is a hammer mill for the local tenants, and BP diesel is on sale.

Crossing another single-lane bridge, visitors arrive outside the Siyendele Community Primary School. Another rusted sign proclaims the Mahlangatsha Rural Development area.

Keeping left, skirt the Thandanani market and enter an agricultural district. There is no wilderness left here and sadly, the land is being rapidly destroyed. Already erosion and the sandy result of leaching are visible. At Ngwempisi R.D.A. Hammer Mill is a government cattle stockyard and plunge dip.

There is a small bridge over the Ngwenpisi river, which leads past the Mabovini Farmers Association and into the hill village of Mankayane.

MANKAYANE

Surrounded by valleys, mountains and forests, Mankayane is a pleasant and quiet settlement. Most places of interest to visitors can be found in the large gravel area in front of the Emvuleni Restaurant and Bar. In Mankayane you will also find Standard Chartered Bank and Total, BP and Shell fuel stations. At the Mankayane Supply Store, a fairly good range of groceries can be purchased. Vegetable and fruit sellers market their wares near the Coca Cola depot. The Text Book Centre has a surprisingly small selection of actual books, but has other things available. Ask the store assistant for handicrafts. Not always on display, these pieces of grasswork and pottery will soon be fetched for viewing.

A frequent bus and taxi service operates from Mankayane. They gather in the open area in front of Emvuleni. At least four buses travel south to Sicunusa, but the majority run north, towards Malkerns, Mbabane, Matsapha and Manzini. Most of the very early morning and late evening buses turn at Loyengo for the timber mill at Bhunya. The first bus north departs from Mankayane at about 7h00. Scroll boards are not dependable and you should ask drivers their destinations – remember to confirm the answer with a few passengers. Hitchhiking north from Mankayane is quick and easy. Getting a lift from Mankayane will usually be in a vehicle going to one of the major centres of Mbabane, Matsapha or Manzini. Private drivers do not seem to expect payment for the lift.

Accommodation in Mankayane is severely limited. While there is a hotel, it is much better and healthier to ask for permission to camp in the grounds of the Elim Free Evangelical Assemblies. A single hotel serves Mankayane.

Near B.K.'s Motor Spares and opposite Lomdhindza Driving School is the well concealed Inyatsi Inn Hotel. For what it offers, it could be classed in the high tariff category. Beds are provided in dirty rooms. A visitor needs to be really beleaguered to seek shelter at the Inyatsi Inn. Hot water is nonexistent and electricity goes off without warning. There are nevertheless hints of past allure in the old buildings. Not recommended to even the hardiest of travellers – unless armed with powerful insecticide and a plastic sheet – consider continuing another 38 km north, to the wide selection of accommodation in the Ezulwini valley. Reservations are never necessary. If for some reason you have to stay at the hotel, bookings can be made.

Address: Inyatsi Inn Hotel, P.O.Mankayane, Mankayane, Swaziland.
Telephone: (09268) 88244.

Mankayane's main attraction is its location for hikes. Leave your transport at the RSP (police) station, north of town. Following any of the highland paths will take you through forests to waterfalls and remote villages. Direction can be disconcerting in the woods, and walkers are advised to get a topographical map and compass before setting off.

Mankayane Hospital lies near an egret's nesting colony. With the nearness of city hospitals, Mankayane Hospital is seldom used by foreign visitors, but basic medical assistance is available.

The rusted and forlorn Mankayane Park entrance is barely visible in the long grass at the edge of the road.

Tall eucalyptus trees line the road from Mankayane. Warning signs advise drivers of difficult conditions ahead. Usutu Pulp Forests have planted the flora on these high hills. Fire watchtowers poke their heads from a world of pine and gum trees. Through humming forests and beautiful remote valleys the road carries travellers north-east, taking an amazing route of close to 45-degree ascents and descents. The valley floor is alluvial and yields good returns on maize crops that are planted annually. A sign to Rosecraft points right to the well-known handicraft centre 18 km away.

An excellent selection of mohair and woollen products is available. The entire operation is carried out on site and visitors can watch the crafters at work. From spinning and weaving to knitting, you can see how Swaziland's most successful handicraft centre designs and manufactures its products.

At the turn-off for Rosecraft, travellers will find the Qhubekani Maswati Store and bus stop. To reach Rosecraft, people using public transport or hitchhiking should get off at this bus stop and cross the road, where they will wait for taxi, bus or lift. Very little public transport travels this route and hitchhiking is a better alternative to a long wait.

Continue straight on past the turn-off. Cross the narrow bridge alongside Thembisa Grocery and Ka-Macondza Wholesalers, at which Total fuel can be bought. Cooked chicken, beef and porridge are available from street vendors who sit near the wholesaler's.

There is a T-junction with the tarred road at Ka-Mgilivane Swaziland Utilities Board. A left turn takes you the 21 forested kilometres to Bhunya. Turning right instead, drivers should observe the 60 km/h speed limit into Loyengo. St Christopher's looms up, followed quickly by the University of Swaziland's Faculty of Agriculture. The campus is off limits to casual visitors. Further north, visitors can visit the Malkerns Agricultural Research Station.

This is a busy road. Mvangati Grocery store also sells BP fuel, while fresh farm produce can be purchased at Takitsi Farm Produce. To the north, surrounded by pineapple fields, is Malkerns and the end of the southern route.

The southern route can easily be completed in a weekend in a saloon car. Albeit not recommended in the rainy season, it is a good introductory tour to Swaziland. A tour of southern Swaziland will lay a foundation for longer, more adventurous trips to remoter areas of the country.

8 CENTRAL ROUTE

Sandlane – Bhunya – Mhlambanyatsi – Malkerns – Matsapha – Manzini
– Siphofaneni – Big Bend – Mpaka Station – Helehele – Manzini
Distance: about 320 km

SANDLANE

Sandlane is really only a border crossing. There are a few houses situated downhill from the South Africa/Swaziland border, but they are
not the traditional settlements visitors will see further inland. Khoisan
paintings can be found in caves north of Sandlane near the start of the
Mponono river. These caves are worth a visit. To avoid the fee required
for a tour group outing, speak to the minister at the Apostolic church,
downhill from the BP Litchfield garage. He is a jovial man who will
call one of the children to guide you for a few Lilangeni. He is also
willing to allow visitors to park vehicles at the church. It is a fairly
strenuous walk if you take the child-guide option, but it gives visitors
the opportunity of meeting rural Swazi people. Leave a small donation
at the church.

If arriving with your own transport, there is no need to get fuel in
Sandlane; there are literally hundreds of filling stations throughout the
tiny kingdom. Visitors travelling through Swaziland by public transport
should wait on the road in front of the church. There are frequent buses
leaving from Sandlane: either to Mbabane via Mhlambanyatsi or further
east to Manzini via Malkerns. Hitchhiking from Sandlane can be difficult as most of the private transport is usually full of passengers and
baggage already. Most hitchhikers end up catching a bus, which apart
from being cheap, is the perfect way to immerse yourself in the adventure that is Swaziland.

East of Sandlane, the tarred road winds across low hills, whose red
soils are cultivated in dramatic contours. About 5 km further, at Inyoni
(Place of Birds), the road descends into conifer forests. This is only the
fringe of one of the largest man-made forests in the world, the majestic
Usutu forests. Once into the forest, visitors find themselves travelling
through a scented green corridor. The effect of being at sea is heightened

Swaziland Central Route

MOZAMBIQUE

Simunye

Mhlumeni

Lonhlopheko

Siteki

Tikuba

HLANE
GAME RESERVE

Hlane

Lukhula

Big Bend

Buckharj

Mpaka stn

Croydon

Miiba

Ngolola

Swaziland
collenes.

MKHAYA NATURE
RESERVE

Siphofaneni

Sithobela

Luve

Mafutseni

Helehele

*LIBETSE
MTS*

*NYONGANE
884*

MUCCUCENE RANGE

Manzini

Ngwane
Park

*SINCENI
MTS*

Forbes Reef

Motshane

Ezulwini

Kwaluseni

Matsapha

Sidvokodvo

Grand Valley

Ngwenya

Mbabane

*MDZIMBA
1 494*

Lobamba

Loyengo

*MAHLANGATSHA
HILLS*

MLILWANE
WILDLIFE SANCTUARY

Malkerns

Mankayane

Oshoek.

Lundzi

Bhunya

*LAPANDA
1 382*

Sicunusa

*HLABENIKOP
1 387*

Mhlambanyatsi

Sandlane

*MBULUNGENI
HILLS*

Houdkop

Waverley

Nerston

SOUTH
AFRICA

as you travel over numerous hills, down into dark wooded valleys, then up onto crests where you can see across the trees that seem to go on to the horizon.

With an estimated 103 600 hectares under planted forests, almost 20 per cent of Swaziland's entire territory is given over to one of her most lucrative export enterprises. While forests are also planted in the north – around Pigg's Peak in the Peak Forest, and a small enclave near the village of Gege in the south – it is the giant Usutu forests, which cover nearly 68 000 hectares and spread in three sweeping prongs around Bhunya, that are Swaziland's pride.

Drivers should be particularly cautious of the large trucks that use this road. Especially dangerous are the timber carriers which, as well as being slow, frequently lose logs from their load. Keep a safe distance from these monsters and overtake as soon as possible. Other offenders along this road are the enormous coal trucks bringing high-grade coal from the mines at Ermelo in South Africa.

Just 7 km from the border is a military training camp on the left. Set in an open area full of boulders and wildflowers with panoramic vistas, this is an incongruous setting for such a place. Cattle also appear to favour this area, and visitors need to be wary of strays on the road – keep your speed low in mist and rain when the animals enjoy lying on the warmer tar.

Next is the Mangcongco Store, which sells a South African manu-factured selection of sweets and city-baked bread. Beyond the store is a tidy collection of buildings which make up the local primary school, and in whose ground campers can pitch their tents during school hol-idays. From the school, the road passes through a number of deep valleys until reaching the trading store at Holnek. Between Holnek and the turn-off onto the gravel road for Mankayane, travellers may see vervet monkeys on the edges of the road. Obviously used to motor vehicles, these monkeys wait patiently for someone passing to throw them a titbit of food. They often dash out in front of vehicles, perform a sort of dance and then rush back to the grass where they sit grinning.

Visitors will occasionally see isolated houses set back from the road, in openings in the forest. These houses are home to the Forest Con-trollers or managers. Living their quiet lives within the trees, they are friendly and hospitable. Should you wish to try camping overnight in the forest, these are the people to ask. They manage "blocks" of trees which cover several hundred hectares, and will gladly grant you per-mission – provided it is not winter and the fire season.

Lookout towers dot the landscape, rising like periscopes to peer out over the ocean of trees. During the dry season, men stand lonely vigil in these towers, straining their eyes for the faintest wisp of smoke, which could signal destruction and death for wildlife and vegetation.

About 2 km east of the turn-off for Mankayane, the road commences a long descent towards the factory town of Bhunya. This is a difficult road, slippery when wet due to the mushy wood slivers and spilled truck oil which accumulates on corners. There is a noticeable temperature change as you drop from the misty heights into the deep valley through which the Lusutfu river flows. The conifers of the high hills give way to wild bananas and tall grasses, which hide the traffic-warning signs on the steep gradient down to Bhunya and the bridge over the Lusutfu river.

BHUNYA

Bhunya is undoubtedly a factory town. The Usutu Pulp Mill, across the river from town, belches polluted smoke into the air. If, however, you decide to brave the pollution and smell, there are a few things worth visiting in and around Bhunya.

Lying in a north-south plan, Bhunya is built to company specifications. There is virtually no random growth within the town, and the feeling of being owned is further enhanced by the boom gates that mark exit and entry points to Bhunya. To get into the interesting area of Bhunya, visitors arriving from Sandlane should take the right turn at the Health Centre and BP Petrol sign as they descend the hill from the south. This tarred road has large speed-humps and passes quaint bus stops. There is no need for those arriving by bus from Sandlane to get off at the entrance to Bhunya as the buses do go into town. At the T-junction, turn left, following the BP signs to the Bhunya branch of the Library Service. Outside the library the road bends left; at which point visitors can either go to the bus and public transport area, or left at the Health Services, towards the suburbs of Bhunya.

Turning left, travellers pass a nursery school. During the week there are always crowds of children gambolling about in the yard, and they delight in meeting visitors while repeating, "'ello, 'ello." Beyond the nursery school, the road climbs to the left, past a cluster of churches. Further up the hill, and around the corner, is one of the suburbs of Bhunya. The church immediately to the right is still used. On Sunday mornings, singing fills the area.

The residents are friendly people, and you will possibly be invited in for a drink.

Continuing down past the Health Services Clinic – at which foreigners in need can find basic treatment – travellers arrive at Bhunya bus depot. This is a fascinating area busy with buses, minibus taxis and street vendors. The street vendors in particular are a vocal bunch, yelling about their wares at the top of their voices. If you have not tried traditional Swazi food, here is an opportunity. Buy some of the stiff maize porridge and beef or goat stew. These curries, which are usually hot, are cheap, tasty and filling.

Most passengers at this bus stop are mill workers on their way to the capital at Mbabane, or the commercial district of Manzini. Around the bus stop you will find the post office, Bhunya fruit and vegetable market, Emazondo Trading Store and loads of local gossip. Buses leave regularly from Bhunya, west to Sandlane, north to Mbabane and east towards Manzini. The buses are well marked, typically Third-World and a lot of fun for adventurous travellers. Those hitching from Bhunya need to walk out of town and onto the main road, then across the bridge, past the Usutu Pulp factory, and choose either the northern or eastern fork in the road. From here, especially going east onto Malkerns and Manzini, there is a great deal of traffic, and you will get a ride quickly.

There are no tourist class hotels. Visitors must either camp in the forests, which have a reputation for being unsafe close to town, or ask at the Evangelical Centre. The centre has a large hall that is used for Christian gatherings, and if it is not in use, the pastor will occasionally allow visitors to sleep there. No fee is asked, but those making use of the pastor's charity should leave a suitable contribution.

Departing Bhunya, turn right at the exit gate and go down to the single-lane bridge over the Lusutfu river. Crossing this bridge can often lead to tense moments as a massive logging truck enters the bridge as you are halfway across. There is no point in arguing with something that size so reverse and wait for him to cross. The on/off ramps on this bridge are terrible. Bus drivers try to avoid the worst parts by racing downhill at top speed, praying that there is nothing on the bridge, and literally skimming across to the other side. Once across the bridge you are directly alongside the mill.

The Usutu Pulp Mill is an ageing monstrosity of noise, pollution and dirt. Around it, the roads are a slippery black mess of timber debris.

Note: This route avoids the heavily used road going from Bhunya east to Malkerns, Ezulwini valley and Manzini. Instead, it follows the road to the left to Mhlambanyatsi and Mbabane.

Along this road, visitors will see a small sign indicating the way to the Forester's Arms Hotel. This is a good tarred road that climbs away from Bhunya back into forests. Mist is frequent on the hilltops.

There are numerous signs advising the prevention of forest fires, a wise warning in this heavily forested area, far from emergency services. Crowned eagles glide effortlessly above the forests and rocky outcrops, searching for elusive meals of hare, rat or other small game. Of special interest to botanists and naturalists are the wild protea that grow on the open hilltops. About 4 km from Bhunya, the road exits a section of forest and climbs to a viewpoint high above the wooded valleys. This is a spectacular place to stop and experience the tranquil stillness of these vast forests.

Travelling north, the road skirts the Mpuluzi High School and Torgyle Central School. The setting of these schools is truly beautiful. It must require a great deal of concentrated effort on the part of the handful of teachers to keep their pupils interested in schoolwork, while nature beguiles them from outside. A mere 12 km from Bhunya is the famous Forester's Arms Hotel; "An hotel built in the forests of paradise," as one South African visitor commented.

Forester's Arms Hotel: High tariff

Located in a clearing of the Usutu forest, the Forester's Arms Hotel is a haven after the oppressiveness of Bhunya. Lying in a mist belt, the hotel nestles beneath towering conifers in an area filled with natural beauty. The owner is an extrovert and happy woman, whose attention to detail has given her hotel a reputation that results in many international organisations using the facility. Visitors will find a wide spectrum of people at the hotel, from the South African family who have driven across the border for the hotel's renowned Sunday lunches, to American and Canadian advisers who work for UNICEF.

Graded as high tariff, the hotel offers visitors an amazing variety of activities and luxuries. The rate includes breakfast, dinner and morning tea or coffee. There are 23 rooms all with en suite bathrooms. A satellite dish brings television programmes from beyond Swaziland's borders. Outdoor types are also catered for. Fishing for bass or trout in the stocked dams is a favourite of many. Permission to fish the rivers and streams of the forest can be obtained either from the Usutu Pulp Company's offices at: Post Office Bag, Mbabane, Swaziland, tel.(09268) 74311, or the Ministry of Agriculture, P.O. Box 162, Mbabane, Swaziland, tel. (09268) 42731.

Lovers of flowers can revel in the fields of arum lilies, agapanthus and heath. Horse riding across the hotel's 585 hectares of wooded wilderness can also be arranged, as can a guided walk to the waterfalls that lie deep in the silence of the dark forests.

Golf is popular with visiting tourists, and a hot-toddy in the English-styled pub is the perfect way to end a game. There is a large clean pool for lazing around and a sauna for the weight watchers who overdid the lavish meals. The dining room is spacious and tastefully decorated. Meals are all prepared on site, with the vegetables grown locally. An extensive menu, buffet and carvery will delight those who enjoy good food. Although prices are high by African standards, the servings and variety will satisfy even the most hungry of guests. Vegetarians should mention this when booking into the hotel. The kitchen staff will then prepare specific meals for you at night – breakfast and lunch are not a problem, with a feast of cereals, fruit and crisp green salads.

Address: Forester's Arms Hotel, P.O. Box 14, Mhlambanyatsi, Swaziland.
Telephone: (09268) 74177, 74377. Fax (09268) 74051.

MHLAMBANYATSI

Further east, travellers arrive at the forestry town of Mhlambanyatsi. Meaning "Watering Place for the Buffalo Soldiers," the town is reputedly named after a regiment of Swazi warriors who stopped here to rest after a particularly gruelling campaign in the eastern Transvaal of South Africa.

The approaches to Mhlambanyatsi are marked by a security control boom and speed-humps. On the road is an Engen fuel garage, for those with their own transport. All along this strip, the road is lined with plane trees which cast fantastic shadows on the road in the late afternoon sun. Travellers hitchhiking or using public transport should get out at the wooden bus shelter in front of Lucky 7 supermarket.

This is another town owned and operated by the Usutu Pulp Company. There is a small shopping centre on Afric Avenue – The Pine Sherwood Cone. The shopping complex houses the Standard Chartered Bank which should be open on Monday, Thursday and Friday from 9h30 to 12h00. It is however often open on a Saturday morning. Visitors wanting to change travellers cheques or draw from credit cards should rather go the extra 27 km to Mbabane for these transactions. Next to the bank is the post office (Eposini). Also in the shopping centre is the office of the Town Clerk, who can provide more information on the history of Mhlambanyatsi, and Lucky 7 supermarket. There is a small informal sector in front of the shopping centre where visitors can buy fruit and vegetables and traditional Swazi meals of maize porridge and meat.

Across the road, to the east of the shopping centre, is the clinic belonging to the company. Near the clinic is a sign to the Mhlambanyatsi Home Industries. This is seldom open over weekends, but visitors should try to see the goods on offer during the week. Remember though, that more traditional Swazi crafts can be bought from the extensive displays in the Ezulwini valley or the remote tribal areas of the country.

A short walk around Mhlambanyatsi will show visitors what can be accomplished with a little care and dedication. The chestnut tree-lined avenues are clean and well maintained, with the air crisp and invigorating. Mhlambanyatsi is in direct contrast to the squalor of Bhunya, a town owned by the same company.

Take the road that dips towards the golf course and airstrip. This road to the Usutu Golf Club is lined with tall, scented gum trees. At the club, visitors will be transported back in time to an age of colonial gentility and indolence. Although the golf course is part of the Usutu Pulp company's facilities, visitors are welcome to take out temporary membership. Enquire at the reception desk. Prior arrangements can be made through the Usutu Pulp Offices, tel. (09268) 74311.

There is no tourist accommodation in Mhlambanyatsi. With the Forester's Arms Hotel, Meikles Mount and hotels of Mbabane all within a few minutes drive of the town, few visitors ever sleep over.

To leave Mhlambanyatsi with your own transport, and continue on this route, turn left back onto the tarred Bhunya-Mbabane road. Buses travelling this route stop for passengers outside the church in Link Lane. Several buses travel daily to Mbabane and back. Hitching from Mhlambanyatsi entails first walking about 1 km out of town, past the security-control boom, and hitching from the open area beyond the boom. Make certain that you hitch from a place where vehicles can pull off the main road.

About 3 km from Mhlambanyatsi, on the right, is the gravel road to Malkerns. The central route will take this road, having first described the road to Mbabane, and then doubling back to this point.

Go straight on into the magnificent valley of the Mhlambanyatsi river. This stretch of road passes through spectacular scenery. Cliffs rise vertically out of the valley floor, forcing the roadbuilders to cut a vein of road from the steep sides. There are openings in the forest, and traditional villages built of mud and thatch cluster beneath exposed rock faces. Outside each settlement, small plots of land are intensively cultivated. Maize, cannabis and sorghum are planted in neat rows and lovingly tended, harvested and enjoyed by these subsistence farmers.

At the Mantabeni General Dealer there is a bus stop, at which travellers wishing to stay at remote Meikles Mount should dismount. It is a daunting walk from the bus stop to the hotel. As there is little traffic likely to pick you up along this road, it is a good idea to start walking. From the quarry, which violently wrenches stone from the hills, it is about 4 km to Meikles Mount. Visitors driving this route should follow the little sign indicating the way to the cottages of Meikles Mount. Travel slowly and in low gear; this is a diabolical road with potholes large enough to swallow a logging truck, never mind a saloon car. In the wet season, getting up to Meikles Mount can be a problem.

Meikles Mount: Medium tariff

Meikles Mount (pronounced Meek-els) lies at the end of a long road in a misty setting of tall trees, hills and cliffs. A wood and thatch gateway marks the entrance, followed by a busy woodyard. You will first have to go past the cottages to the reception office, which is some way from the accommodation. There are seven self-catering thatched cottages made up of a house, five two bedroomed cottages and one singles cottage. All units have fully equipped kitchens, bathroom, patio and dining area. The kitchen facilities are gas fired and need priming before guests arrive. Make certain to book in advance. Electricity comes from a generator which is switched on at night. Gas-fired lamps lend an old-world charm to the cottages. Although the management can occasionally be a little brusque, the sheer natural beauty of the surroundings makes up for any unpleasantness.

There are walking trails through the forested hills and up onto the summit of Mhlane (1341 m). Horse riding, fishing and bird-watching are other activities available, though most guests prefer to laze around the swimming pool and drift away in the tranquil silence. For visitors who wish to stay at Meikles Mount over the Christmas period, it is imperative that you book before October.

Address: Meikles Mount, P.O. Box 13, Mhlambanyatsi, Swaziland.
Telephone: (09268) 74110.

Driving north from the turn-off to Meikles Mount, turn back onto the tarred road, near the clinic and pre-school. Continue along this road, crossing the Mkwebani river with Mkwebani on the left. Between the Stobela and Nondvo rivers, to the right of the main road, is a range of low hills. These hills are peopled with a friendly and hospitable clan who live in close proximity to one another.

There are rock paintings in these hills, and although off the tourist trail, visitors who are prepared to tackle the strenuous walk to the sites can find a guide at Siphocosini village. The shopkeeper at Sizabantu Grocery is helpful and will find you a guide within 15 minutes. Do not take advantage of the natural generosity of these people. They may not ask for any payment but it is good policy to give a donation which will smooth the way for the next travellers who come in search of the paintings.

Proceeding north, a little way beyond Siphocosini, the road passes a soccer field. Matches held there on Saturday afternoons are definitely worth attending. Spectators come from miles around to support their teams. The natural exuberance of the Swazis is given free rein at these games, and it is extremely difficult not to get caught up in the excitement.

Travellers next reach Luphohlo dam. Built in a cup of sandstone hills, the dam gouges a wedge out of the valley. The Mbabane Boat Club is also located at the dam, and visitors who would like to participate in boating, should speak to the person on duty. Camping is allowed around the dam. Should you decide to camp at Luphohlo it is advisable to leave the main park and recreation area and go up into the surrounding hills. You will need to bring all your own equipment and food for the duration of your stay. Gorges and natural forests provide a wonderful setting for a pitch and the honesty and friendliness of the people make it a safe proposition.

Leaving Luphohlo dam, continue north, across the Lusushwana river (which feeds into the dam) and the Luphalwane river, before reaching All-Saints primary school.

On either side of the Amanzimyana river are steep cliffs that provide challenging but technically simple climbs for those who want to pit their skills against the rock. It is, however, a brittle rock and only experienced rock climbers with adequate equipment should attempt the higher and more dangerous ascents.

From the bridge over the Amanzimyana river, the road enters an area of forests again but with a noticeable change in the materials used in house building. Traditional techniques using mud, wood and thatch are replaced by concrete blocks and shiny, corrugated iron roofs. People also become less interested in meeting foreigners and are more sophisticated. At the settlement of Hill Top, a traffic circle allows access to the Mbabane road and to the roads going down the Ezulwini valley to Manzini. While there is not much in the way of attractions to tourists in Hill Top, the Hill Top Bottle Store has ice-cold beer and cold-drinks, which make an addition to the fried snacks that the street vendors hawk near the circle.

Retracing your route past the Luphohlo dam, Siphocosini and Meikles Mount to the gravel road turn-off for Malkerns, is about 27 km. Turn left onto the good gravel road and enter the forests of Usutu Pulp again. Mist often occurs over these hills and deep valleys. The road is frequently used by motorists, and hitchhikers will have little trouble getting a lift through to Malkerns, about 19 km away. Only two buses travel this route and travellers using public transport may have to hitch. A combination of hitching and walking is the most enjoyable way of travelling along this short cut to the pineapple growing area of Malkerns.

About 2 km along this road is a Y-junction. Take the left fork for Qwabitsi, Malkerns, Manzini. The right fork goes to the forestry airstrip. As the road continues further towards Malkerns, conifers are grown right to the very edge of the gravel. It is an eerie passage through a green forest full of pine scent and bird-song. From Qwabitsi, there are impressive views down into the Malkerns valley and over the hundreds of hectares of pineapples. There is a dramatic drop from the misty highland hills and forests to Malkerns. Few fences line the road, and visitors pass through pineapple fields. The area is famed for growing the Swazi Queen canning pineapple. The climate is noticeably warmer. Tourism has made large inroads around Malkerns, but few people take time to explore the town itself, preferring the curio shops that line the main Bhunya-Manzini road. Where the gravel road reaches the tar, turn left into the agricultural settlement of Malkerns.

MALKERNS

Straddling the tarred road from Bhunya, Malkerns lies in a north-east to south-west plan. Malkerns is another town that grew up around an agricultural-orientated enterprise. Its main attractions to visitors are its splendid location and the pineapple production. Around town, fields of growing pineapples can be seen pushing their spiky fruit into the air. Travelling into Malkerns from the gravel road, you will pass the Malkerns Wine, Malt and Beer shop. This is a gathering place for many of the town's older residents. If you are prepared to sit awhile, they enjoy telling stories, in broken English, of what they have seen happen in their beautiful valley.

North is St Anne's High School, the interesting shopping centre and Caltex fuel garage. The Royal Swaziland Police are across from St John Bosco Primary School. They are friendly officers, and will look after your vehicle while you walk around exploring their town. Master Cleaners are across the road, and will do a good job of cleaning your clothes – most articles of laundry can be collected the next day.

For a good introduction to the food of this area, try a meal at the fascinating Mangozeni Restaurant. With a dingy interior, it will instantly transport visitors into the life of Third-World working people. Another place for getting to meet the locals is the Ekuthuleni Bar.

Travellers arriving or leaving by bus will find transport in the open sandy area in front of Macembe Store. This region is well served by buses, although the destinations written on their scrolls are often different to their actual destinations. Should you miss the bus at this stop, make a dash for the other bus stop next to St Anne's School. The bus usually has to go and get fuel anyway.

Near the bus stop is a busy and interesting hawkers market. You will find the most unusual things for sale; from a bushel of fresh tomatoes to a calf's head. Squeamish visitors should rather avoid this market, but for the stout-hearted, it is a must.

Sadly, around these shops is an area of abysmal poverty. Children play in fetid water puddles, smoke from cooking fires makes the eyes water, and piles of paper, plastic and tin make a depressing sight.

Further along, across from Phakama General Store and Ekuthuleni Bar, are the post office and Standard Chartered Bank. Malkerns Country Club is near Pep stores, and is the centre for the farmers and managers of the pineapple estates. Tennis courts can be hired at the country club. Check telephonically if courts are available. Tel. (09268) 83018.

Between Pep Stores and the National Health Services clinic, is the main employer of the Malkerns district: Swazican Swaziland Fruit Canners. The factory is involved in canning and jam making.

From Malkerns, follow the destination boards for Manzini and the smaller sign for Swazi Candles. If walking to Swazi Candles, go through the wooden marketplace, past the mud and tin houses up onto the main road, then left for about 1 km. Drivers should turn left out of Malkerns, then continue past Esibuyeni Bar to the Malkerns Church sign, where you can turn right to Swazi Candles.

Before entering the candle workshop, go across to the open-air carving site beneath the trees. Quiet men chop and sand away at beautiful wooden sculptures, singing softly as they work. You may choose from animist masks, animals and tribal scenes cut from logs.

The first thing that will strike visitors to Swazi Candles is the explosion of colour. Swazi Candles is unique to Africa. Started by whites, it is run almost entirely by local Swazis now. Should you decide to buy a candle, be warned that they are not cheap. All major credit cards are accepted. For travellers on a tight budget, spend a few minutes going through the "seconds," which are just as good as the "first" works, but at a reduced price.

A visit to Swazi Candles is a must. The warm wax smells, loud music and creative atmosphere will delight even the most pessimistic of visitors. Details regarding mass purchases, trade inquiries and other information about Swazi Candles can be obtained either by writing, telephoning or via fax.

Address: Swazi Candles, P.O. Box 172, Malkerns, Swaziland.
Telephone: (09268) 83219. fax (09268) 83135.

Buses will stop to pick up travellers on the main road outside Swazi Candles. Lifts are also easy to get from here, as the road is heavily used and you should not have to wait longer than 15 minutes. Visitors with their own vehicles should leave Swazi Candles and turn right in a north-east direction. Follow the signboard for Baobab Batik Shop, where even batik postcards can be bought. Next to the batik shop is Nyanza Gem Shop. Gems and geological specimens from all over Swaziland can be found in this little shop. Exquisite animist ritual masks are also available. Ask any of the women who sit beneath the trees outside the shop. If you are not going further east into the tribal lands, this is a good place to pick up a genuine piece of Swazi art. Included in the gem shop is a tiny book exchange in which travellers will be able to find a selection of paperbacks in several languages. Behind the batik factory is Nyanza Stables, from where visitors can explore the area with a guide and docile mount.

Across the road from Nyanza Gem Shop is Emangweni Farm Produce, an excellent place to stock up on fresh fruit and vegetables – so fresh that many of the items are still attached to soil clods. Next to the fresh produce shop is Tinkukhu Poultry Farm and Road Stall. Eggs and chicken can be bought here. The woman who sells at the stall often has a delicious chicken curry available (no rice, but hot maize porridge instead.)

From Tinkukhu Poultry Farm, the road climbs to a Y-junction. Travellers who are following this route should proceed along the right fork, towards Manzini. A few kilometres north-east is a T-junction. Hitchhikers and those using public transport will find the road here an absolute delight to travel. There is a constant stream of buses and other traffic. With the renowned hospitality of the Swazi, you will soon be ensconced in someone's car or among a crowd of friendly, talkative bus passengers.

At the T-junction, turn right, along the road going to Manzini. Across to the right, you will notice the grotesque shapes of mining equipment in the rock quarry slashed from the once pristine Swazi landscape. Proceed past the sign for the National Agricultural Marketing Board to Sheba Handweavers, on the left of the road. Here visitors will find a good selection of rugs, tapestries and wall-hangings. A lot of diligent creativity goes into these fine pieces of work, which have become famous across southern Africa.

Next is the Republic of China's Agricultural Mission. Litchi orchards and cereal crops fill the fields around the mission. During harvest season, travellers are able to buy fruit from many of the roadside sellers.

High Hope Riding Stables is off the road, a few metres east of the Salt 'n Pepper Club (where the locals rave on weekend nights). This is also the site of Swaziland's only registered horse stud. Lessons, stabling and short rides can be arranged at High Hope. It is advisable to book well ahead, especially over the festive season and on long weekends.

Address:　　High Hope Stables, P.O. Box 47, Manzini, Swaziland.
Telephone: (09268) 84364/52317.

Once across the Matsapha river, travellers enter the industrial and international airport town of Matsapha. Unless going to the airport, or particularly keen on industrial estates, there is no reason why a visitor should want to visit Matsapha. If you are waiting for a plane however, you might as well spend a few hours walking about the suburbs and business areas of town.

MATSAPHA

Established in 1968, Matsapha is the centre for Swaziland's industrial estates. Over 80 per cent of all industry in Swaziland is within the magisterial district of Matsapha.

As you enter town, the first built-up area you come to is a shopping complex. While most buses and taxis go all the way to the airport, you can get off here. The shopping complex has most places that will be of importance to visitors.

The Total fuel garage is a good place to ask around for lifts if you are hitchhiking out of Matsapha. If having trouble with your own vehicle, visit the spares shop near the garage. The counter attendants are helpful and courteous, and will even locate a cheap mechanic if you need repairs done to your vehicle. The same complex houses the Royal Swazi Police.

Lamabota Takeaways has a typically American menu as well as the more traditional meals of beef or chicken stew. Royal Swazi Airlines also has an office here, but it is only a branch office and you should book your ticket or make enquiries in Mbabane. There is a small well-stocked chemist, Pep stores and an efficient branch of the Union Bank. Kentucky Fried Chicken is fast and clean, while next door, the fully licensed Las Cabanas Restaurant offers a diverse menu. Reservations are seldom necessary. Tel. (09268) 84130.

East of the shopping complex is a Shell fuel station and Swaziland Brewers. Tours of the brewery are offered. The tour is well guided and informative. Bookings are essential and it is advised that you add your name to the list at least 10 days in advance. Tel. (09268) 86033 or fax (09268) 86309. For detailed information, which is readily available, write to the Human Resources Manager, Swaziland Brewers, P.O. Box 539, Manzini, Swaziland.

Leaving the shopping complex, turn right, past the fuel station, and follow the signs for Matsapha railway station. This road will take you into the heart of Matsapha's industrial estates.

Many fuel stations line the road to the airport, which also passes the Royal Swaziland Police's training college. The airport is about 5 km from town, on a windy ridge dominated by the periscopic eye of the control tower. Enquiries about flights can be obtained from the airport information desk, tel. (09268) 84451. Car hire is available directly from the airport, through Hertz/Imperial or Avis. Hertz/Imperial: Tel. (09268) 84393. Avis: tel. (09268) 52734.

Several buses and minibus taxis provide transport to and from Mbabane and Manzini. Ask the minibus taxi price before taking a ride, and make certain you understand their exact destination.

There is a flying club at the airport; Swaziland Flying Club, P.O. Box 487, Manzini, Swaziland. Tel. (09268) 84372.

At the Cheshire Home near the Swaziland Bottling Company in the industrial estate disabled people make a range of handicrafts. Visitors are welcome to walk around the facility. Reservations are not necessary. If you want to aid Cheshire Homes having returned home, they can offer suggestions. Tel. (09268) 55241/86334.

There is no point in trying to find accommodation in Matsapha. With Manzini less than 10 km away, most people search there for a place to sleep.

To leave Matsapha and continue on the central route, drivers should turn in front of the Shell garage, back onto the new road going to Manzini. Hitchhikers will find it difficult leaving Matsapha. Constructors are busy on the MR3 highway and there is nowhere a vehicle can pull off. Rather take a bus or taxi from the airport to Manzini.

Entering the Mbabane-Manzini road, continue past Ndlunganye General Dealer and the street vendors who sell fruit and vegetables. Behind the street vendors is the turning for the southern urban centre of Nhlangano (See southern route.) Carry straight on for Manzini. Observe the 60 km/h speed limit along this section of road.

From Matsapha to Manzini there is no break in housing, shops and buildings. Children frequently play in the road and cows that have broken loose from their tethers graze contentedly along the road verge. A set of traffic lights signifies the entrance to Manzini, and the speed limit drops to 30 km/h. If not stopping in Manzini, drive along Ngwane Road through town, round the traffic circle near the Manzini Club, and follow the route indicators for Siteki.

Most budget travellers using public transport or hitchhiking will have to get off in Manzini. Unless you have had the good fortune to get a through ride, or caught a bus directly from Mbabane, you will have to change in Manzini.

MANZINI

Located close to the geographical centre of Swaziland, Manzini is known as the "hub of the nation." At the time of British rule, Manzini was the administrative capital of Swaziland. Even though the government has now moved nearer to Mbabane, Manzini still retains jurisdiction of the large Manzini province. Industry and commerce are the main enterprises in this, Swaziland's second largest urban centre. Manzini is famous for the annual Trade Fair held at the end of August and early September.

Lying in a west-east plan, Manzini clusters in a long shallow valley about 8 km east of Matsapha. Entering from Matsapha, visitors travel along the main tarred road, across the Umzimnene river, and up past the showgrounds of Swaziland's International Trade Fair. From the showgrounds, there is a curving rise in the road until the corner of Mhlakuvane and Ngwane Roads. Ngwane Road is a one-way from west to east through town.

There are two roads of importance to visitors: Ngwane and Nkose-luhlaza. On Ngwane Road visitors will find the library, numerous modern shops, office blocks and fast-food restaurants. Along Nkoseluhlaza Road is the post office, on the same block as the RSP (police). Visit one of the country's greatest markets, on the corner of Mancishana and Mhlakuvane Roads.

Good tourist information can be obtained by contacting the desk at the Curriculum Centre. Follow Meintjies Road to the T-junction near the Central School. Turn left here, then right, to the centre. The staff are friendly and have a wealth of information about Manzini and the surrounding area, including hotel accommodation and places to eat.

Fuel is available from filling stations around town; those along Ngwane and Nkoseluhlaza are efficient and convenient. The main bus and minibus taxi depot is opposite the Mocambique Motel and Restaurant. The women who work in the motel can assist travellers with information on bus times. Hitchhiking out of Manzini presents problems. Traffic cannot stop within the city centre and it is unlikely that you will get a lift to your destination from town. Instead, walk east from town. Continue past the traffic circle, west of the Manzini Club, and get to the area outside the golf course. Here you have a choice of lifts: east towards Siteki or south to Big Bend.

Manzini is besieged by touts who try to steer you towards places that will pay them commission. It also suffers from dramatic price increases during the Trade Fair. The most popular tourist-class accommodation is found in town or within a few kilometres of the CBD.

Mocambique Motel and Restaurant: Medium tariff

This motel is located on Mahleko Road, near the public transport depot. Rooms are comfortable and all have air conditioning. Most of the guests are businessmen, either enjoying the well-prepared meals in the restaurant or relaxing in the busy bar. Visitors who enjoy seafood should take advantage of the fare available in the restaurant. Particularly good are the king and queen prawns with a variety of side dishes. Few travellers actually stay at the motel, but a meal here is recommended. Reservations are not necessary for the motel, but for a table in the restaurant bookings must be made ahead of time. For guests who prefer prior arrangements, contact the motel manager.

Address: Mocambique Motel and Restaurant, P.O. Box 417, Manzini, Swaziland.
Telephone: (09268) 52489.

The New George Hotel: High tariff

Serving a large number of the expatriate community in Manzini, the New George Hotel is expensive, modern and incredibly snooty. Even though a high fee is charged, visitors should not count on a high standard of service in return. Not 1 km from the colonial world of the Manzini Club, tennis and golf can be arranged – but not through the hotel. You will have to make your own bookings. Contact the club manager at the Manzini Club on Siteki Road, tel. 52254.

All 55 rooms have en suite bathrooms, television and air conditioning. A swimming pool is also available. An à la carte restaurant has an extensive wine list and a good selection of meals. Vegetarians have little to choose from though, and it is advisable to contact the hotel manager on arrival. The pub is crowded, loud and comfortable. Bookings are requested.

Address: The New George Hotel, P.O. Box 51, Manzini, Swaziland.
Telephone: (09268) 52061, fax 52061.

Budget travellers and visitors who are willing to scout around will have no trouble finding suitable accommodation. There are rooms and small family-run inns that are seldom advertised and not mentioned in locally written books.

Highway Motel: Medium to low tariff

Out along the motorway, east of the Manzini Club, is the Highway Motel. With a bar and nightclub filled with locals, this is worth considering. It is not a First-World place but a real Swazi dive. People are friendly and keen to meet visitors. It is not required that you book ahead, but it can be an advantage, especially over public holidays and the festive season. If you telephone them from the bus depot they will arrange a taxi to come and collect you – meaning that you will not have to deal with the touts.

Cheap meals are also available, but the menu is limited. Visitors can bring their own food, which will be prepared for you at the motel. To book ahead contact the motel manager.

Address: Highway Motel, P.O. Box 110, Manzini, Swaziland.
Telephone: (09268) 50614.

Accommodation can also be arranged by contacting St Theresa's High School and Convent. It is unlikely that male travellers will be given a bed in the convent but camping is sometimes allowed in the school grounds. No fee is asked, but leave a contribution to aid in the running of this gracious, serene and busy religious centre. Speak to the Mother Superior. Tel. 52519.

To the west, along First Avenue, is the hospital where emergency medical treatment can be obtained. Foreigners are required to first pay the bill, then claim from their medical insurance. The Manzini Club is certainly worth a visit. This is one spot where it seems the British never left. Gin and tonics are still taken in the evenings after a day of tennis or golf.

A shopping mall has recently been built close to the centre of the CBD. The shops are similar to those found in any large town. One place that must be visited is the market on Friday and Saturday mornings. Go west on Nkoseluhlaza Road to Sandlane Road. Turn left here, and then right into Mancishana Road. The market is on the corner of Mhlakuvane Road.

For a real Swazi experience, get to the market just before sunrise. The hawkers and vendors arrive in a colourful mass. In the time leading up to about 8h00 there are moments of organised chaos. Fresh fruit and vegetables, trinkets, cooked food, curios and clothing are all neatly laid out for prospective customers. Then, at about 7h45, there is a pause before the shoppers arrive. Unlike the Mbabane market, there are few tourists here and prices are accordingly lower. Bargaining is accepted practice and will result in hilarious moments as communication breaks down due to language difficulties.

Leaving Manzini east from the traffic circle, alongside the Manzini Club golf course, travellers will pass the Moneni Supermarket, Caltex fuel garage and Shangri-la Dairy. By this stage the low speed limit of town will have been replaced by an 80 km/h limit. Past the dairy, about 8 km from Manzini at Helehele, is the well-known Gobble 'n Gossip Restaurant. Besides serving the most scrumptious pub lunches, the restaurant offers the opportunity of meeting the locals, who can usually be found in the beer garden over weekends. An à la carte menu is also available.

East of the Gobble 'n Gossip Restaurant is a turning to the right, to the sugar growing district of Big Bend. It is 38 km to Siphofaneni and 60 km to Big Bend, all on an excellent tarred road. If hitchhiking from Helehele, walk about 500 m along the Big Bend road before starting to hitch. Many of the vehicles that congregate at the junction are coming or going from the neighbourhood. Travellers using buses should do the same thing, then flag down a bus that takes the turning. It is important to ask where your lift or bus is going, and if hitchhiking, to find out whether a fare is expected.

Even on this well maintained road, the speed limit remains at 80 km/h. On many sections of the road to Big Bend, the road markings were apparently created by someone who was either blind or had never driven a vehicle. Solid white no overtaking lines appear on perfectly straight open roads, while broken overtaking lines are painted on blind rises and corners. With caution and discretion, drivers should rather make their own interpretation of the road markings. Visitors using this route will immediately begin to notice a change in the vegetation as they leave the area around Helehele and Manzini. The mist, tall trees and lush green growth start to give way to a drier more savanna-like region. Modern houses are replaced by traditional mud, wood and thatch huts. Vistas of wide plains become more frequent the further southeast you travel.

From Mphosi Store you can see the distant Lebombo mountains to the east. Before Gilgal Secondary School are a series of speed humps that many drivers don't see until it is too late. The hills of western Swaziland begin to recede and by the time you reach Phonjwane or stop for fuel at Vikizijula Grocery store, you will be in an area of flat grassland and acacia trees. Roadside sellers sell wood and grass baskets. The baskets are locally made, cheap and make good gifts. Some of the more modern houses seem to be used by graffiti artists who spray away with vigour and colour. One particularly baffling scrawl reads: House of Exile. The house is empty and has a forgotten air.

Siphofaneni is a small settlement on the banks of the Lusutfu river. Visitors who stop here usually do so for the fishing. Fishing permits are necessary and can be obtained from the Ministry of Agriculture, P.O. Box 162, Mbabane, Swaziland. Tel. (09268) 42731. It has a Shell garage and the Nkambule Shopping Centre (which is a Swazi-style supermarket). The Kanok Thula Restaurant usually has a crowd of local youths lounging around outside. Inside it's dark and intriguing, but with the cold beer and hot chicken stew it serves, you quickly begin to feel at ease.

A bakery on the outskirts of town, near the RSP (police), bakes bread each morning and you can buy a loaf from the front office. Very few buses only go as far as Siphofaneni; most carry on to Big Bend or Manzini. The bus drivers spend a few minutes outside the Shell garage waiting for passengers. Ask them to hoot when it is time to leave. They are accommodating men who are quite happy to stop at points of interest for travellers.

Hitchhikers need to walk to the outskirts of the settlement, and wait beyond the Siphofaneni Primary School – where you are certain to have a lively reception during term time.

Once past the sugar irrigation schemes on the right, travellers will be out in the bush. Villages are further apart here and people walk long distances to collect water. Dry riverbeds, thorn trees and erosion characterise the landscape. Small, carefully cultivated plots are hemmed in by barricades of thorn branches to keep out marauding goats and cattle. A little church is tucked in near Magidzela Store.
The entrance to Mkhaya Game Reserve is on the left.

Mkhaya Game Reserve: High tariff

This reserve, in the lowlands of eastern Swaziland, has a unique place in the world's fight to save endangered species. It was founded in 1979 to promote the survival of the disappearing Nguni cattle of southern Africa. So successful was this undertaking that sufficient funds were generated to allow looking at other endangered species on the continent.

Today, Mkhaya is in the forefront of the battle to propagate the rare black rhino. Its anti-poaching squads are world renowned for their effectiveness and dedication. Yet there is more to Mkhaya than just black rhino; each aspect of conservation is treated as vital. Highly trained game rangers accompany visitors on a variety of walks and drives. The approach is not solely animal orientated; grasses, birds, reptiles and aquatic life are handled in an entirely holistic way.

Accommodation is provided in cottages and furnished tents. Prices are all in the high-tariff category, but visitors should remember that this reserve is privately owned and relies heavily on guest support.

If you are just passing through, or on a really tight budget, consider one of the day tours. Guided jeep trips begin at 10h00 and finish at about 16h00, with lunch included in the price. By far the most exciting thing to do is to take part in the one day rafting trip down the Lusutfu river. These trips are run in the warm months between December and April. Not only is this a wonderful way to see the African bush and game, but moments of adrenalin-pumping excitement will leave you breathless and keen to try the white-water rapids again.

Evenings are languid and relaxing, with supper prepared in traditional pots on open fires. Meat is the main ingredient and visitors who are vegetarians should inform the senior hostess upon arrival. The staff are accommodating and well trained, meaning that nearly everything you try at Mkhaya is a memorable experience. After supper, a night drive into the darkness and noises of the bush, or watching a tribal Sibhaca dance, are the ideal ways to finish a stay at Mkhaya.

Reservations are necessary well in advance. Camping can usually be arranged on arrival or a day in advance.

Address: Big Game Parks of Swaziland Holdings, Central Reservation Office, P.O. Box 234, Mbabane, Swaziland, or at their physical address: 1st Floor, Dhlan'ubeka House, corner Tin and Walker St, Mbabane.
Telephone: (09268) 45006, fax (09268) 44246.

Leaving Mkhaya is seldom a problem. Hitchhikers should ask around at the camps or wait where the gravel road from the reserve intersects the tarred road between Siphofaneni and Big Bend. Buses travel the route throughout the day, and can be flagged down from the same place.

South-east from Mkhaya Game Reserve, travellers will pass Mamphlo Grocery, which sells an assortment of sweets, vegetables, alcohol and fresh bread. There is a steady increase in cultivation from Tambuti Estate Fruit Stall. The silence of the bush is replaced by the stutter of irrigation sprinklers. High game fencing surrounds citrus groves. Sugar fields begin to crowd into the shallow valleys, the hill tops dotted with fever trees. A Ministry of Health Malaria Centre is situated along this road, and although not always open, can be visited when it is. The staff are talkative and will explain their techniques and treatments for dealing with the malaria carrying mosquitoes.

Dense groves belonging to Tambuti Citrus Estates continue to hide behind high fences until the road passes the Hendrik van Eck dam on the right. Beyond the dam, the road curves alongside the giant sugar mill, with the Lebombo mountains to the east. A sign points the way to Big Bend just before an irrigation canal.

BIG BEND

Situated in the middle of an enormous sugar-growing area, Big Bend is one of the largest centres along the eastern frontier. Getting its name from the wide bend made by the meandering Lusutfu river, Big Bend lies in a north-south plan.

Dominated by Ubombo Ranches' sugar mill, Big Bend is undoubtedly a company town (like many other towns in Swaziland). Tucked in below the Lebombo mountains and the wide plains of eastern Swaziland, it resembles an oasis in the browns of the bush. Follow the road sign which points to Big Bend. Visitors cross a causeway over an irrigation canal. On Friday and Saturday afternoons, buses are washed alongside this canal and it is a sight to be seen. Children strip down to their birthday suits and joyfully plunge into the slow-moving green waters of the canal. Hoisting out buckets, they splash the sides of the buses. Moving in behind the children are the drivers. Armed with brooms and mops, they scrub the dirt, mud and oil from their African queens. With sunset throwing a mantle of gold over the mountains and the gentle colours of Swaziland, a thousand photo opportunities are created.

Passing along hedges of orange and purple bougainvillea, you will encounter the Ubombo Ranches offices. Tours of the mill and some of the surrounding sugar estates can be arranged during the week. This is a fascinating trip. Conservationists and environmentalists should also try one of these tours. You'll be pleasantly surprised at the attempts at conservation that are being made by the company. The guides are informative, courteous and dedicated. Although occasionally you can just turn up at the factory or farm gate and be fortunate enough to join a tour, it is better to apply through the office first.

Address: Ubombo Ranches, P.O. Box 23, Big Bend, Swaziland.
Telephone: (09268) 36511, fax (09268) 36330.
A few hundred metres further south, visitors will find an open area
full of buses, minibus taxis and street vendors. Those arriving by bus
or hitchhiking, should get off here. There are long-distance buses leaving from 6h00 each morning. Hitching from Big Bend is also very easy.
    Many of the street vendors sell sugar cane. This has an interesting
taste but chewing the fibres can be hard on the teeth.
    South of the Ubombo Ranches Private Hospital is Barclay's Bank, a
fuel garage, Lusiba Trading and Pep stores. Emergency treatment for
non-Ubombo employees is available at the hospital but is expensive.
With First-World hospitals across the nearby border in South Africa,
many ill or injured travellers prefer to head for there instead of the
limited treatment of this private hospital.
    Where the town extends over a low hill, south from the hospital, a
gravel road runs between Standard Chartered Bank and a dilapidated
fuel garage. This gravel road winds higher between frangipane and
flame trees, bougainvillea and aloes, until it exits outside the Bend Inn.

Bend Inn: Medium tariff

Known throughout Swaziland, and acclaimed in Ted Simon's best selling travel book, *Jupiter's Travels*, this is the place to stay. Accommodation is provided in 23 rather spartan rooms. Four of the rooms have
baths, while the remainder have showers. An English breakfast is included in the room rate, but can be a problem for vegetarians. Speak
to the manager the evening before about your food preferences. Full
course meals are available in the dining room, and a seafood restaurant
is soon to be opened.
    But, if you decide to stay at the Bend Inn, it will not be for the
accommodation or food. The two main reasons for staying at the Inn
are the view from the pool bar, and the Zoo Bar parties on Saturday
night. Having an evening drink at the pool bar must be one of the most
breathtaking experiences in Swaziland. The view across the wide Lusutfu river, as it winds through sugar fields and Swazi bush, on its way
to the port (poort – colloquially) and Mozambique, is a memorable sight.
Warm, grass scented breezes drift up from the valley, while the drone
of "expat" conversations lends a colonial atmosphere to the whole
setting.
    On Saturday night, after 22h00, the place to be in Big Bend is the
Zoo Bar. People come from kilometres away; in cars, in buses, by bicycle

and on foot. Within hours there is barely any standing room and you'll find the party spilling over into the yard, swimming pool and rooms. It is a festive, peaceful celebration of life. There are snacks, bar meals and drinks, all at a reasonable rate.

Prior reservations for accommodation at the Bend Inn are not necessary, but to be certain, especially over the Christmas season, book a week or two in advance.

Address: Bend Inn, P.O. Box 37, Big Bend, Swaziland.
Telephone: (09268) 36111.

For hikers, walks can be taken into the hills and valleys of the Lebombo mountains east of town. The areas higher up are sparsely populated and you will need to carry all your own food and camping equipment. A challenging but delightful walk can be taken from the Bend Inn. The manager will obligingly allow you to park your car at the inn. Cross the tarred road and go down to the wide sandy banks of the Lusutfu river. Follow the river through the irrigated sugar cane to the start of the poort (ravine) in the mountains.

Where the Nyetane river enters the Lusutfu river, continue straight up the hill. It is a tiring climb to the summit at 651 m but the awesome panorama is certainly worth the aching leg muscles. East of the summit, you can walk downhill to the settlement of Thivili. Few foreigners reach this remote hill village, where the people are still very tribal.

The Ubombo Ranches recreation club and golf course is available for sailors and sportsmen visiting Big Bend. Temporary membership can be obtained by contacting the secretary at the Ubombo Ranches offices, tel. (09268) 36511. Fishing and sailing are available at the Hendrik van Eck dam. For boating, contact the yacht club at the dam. Fishing permits for the dam and river can be obtained from the Ministry of Agriculture, P.O. Box 162, Mbabane, Swaziland, or from the Ubombo Recreation Club for the Hendrik van Eck dam.

Lusiba Trading sells motor spares and carries out basic repairs and services. He is relatively cheap, but not in any hurry, and emergency repairs should rather be referred to Imbabala Motors, tel. 36141. Near the northern entrance to Big Bend, along the gravel road, visitors will find the post office, RSP (police), and the way to the yacht club, Hendrik van Eck dam and the Royal Residence. A quicker route to the post office is to go past the street vendors, near the public toilets, then up onto the road in front of the RSP (police).

A beautiful stroll can be had by walking along the canal that flows sluggishly in front of the Ubombo Primary School. This path winds through tall grass, colourful wildflowers and shady trees. The church, to the right of the path just after the footbridge over the canal, has a good vocal congregation whose singing can be heard on Sundays. Try to get out to the Royal Residence – remember no photography is permitted. If the family is not in residence you may be allowed to take a walk around the residential grounds and certain of the buildings. This provides an insight as to how one of the few monarchies left in Africa live in a mixture of traditional and modern style. To find out whether a visit is possible, write or telephone.

Address: Inkilongo Nkhundla – Royal Residence, P.O. Box 136, Big Bend, Swaziland.
Telephone: (09268) 36281.

About 9 km north-west from Big Bend, past the Hendrik van Eck dam and Mhlosinga Nature Reserve, is the turning to Siteki and Lomahasha. Regular buses travel the route between Big Bend and Siteki. There are two buses in the morning, two in the afternoon and one in the evening. If you miss these buses, it is fairly easy to hitchhike to Siteki or Lukhula, which are on the route to Manzini and Mbabane.

Known as the MR16, this road has recently been tarred and is in good condition. It has a 80 km/h speed limit. From here visitors will begin to see road signs which also show the distance to Maputo in Mozambique.

Cultivated fields soon give way to acacias and fever trees. The bush gets thicker and the natural grass longer. Travellers have now entered one of Swaziland's major cattle-ranching districts. Owned mostly by Ubombo Ranches, these enormous ranches run some of the best beef herds in Africa. Most of the farm managers are friendly and proud to show a visitor around their herds and lands. Observant travellers may spot bateleurs soaring on the warm air currents above the bush, searching their domain for a meal.

Drivers who are using the South African Automobile Association map of Swaziland, dated 8 January 1992, should note that a number of the roads turning off the MR16 are not shown. In addition to this, some of the roads which are included are incorrectly indicated.

There are regular bus stops all along this road, as far as the Jabula Butchery and Café. A cheery fellow runs the store, and happily carries out the work of slaughtering cattle, sheep and goats while also serving customers ice-cold beers or grilled chickens.

The further north visitors travel, the more aware they will become of the tribalness of the settlements. Occasional cotton fields toss up their snow-white fluff, but the bush has crowded out man's efforts at subjection here. After Mpholonjeni Store and Siphoso School – which stands brightly in abandoned cotton lands – there is a turning onto the D4 gravel road. There is a little sign at the turn-off.

I have described this road through the bush to take visitors off the beaten track and into the very heartland of the Swazi. It is an extraordinary journey into tribal Africa, to villages where shamans still chant their mantras to Father Sun and Mother Earth. For those who want to discover the essence of the Swazi nation, this is the route to follow. It is not easy and will demand concentration and perseverance, but nothing else you do in Swaziland will be quite like this route. It can be done by any saloon car, although in the rainy season a 4x4 or motorcycle are the only way.

Obviously, it will present problems to those who do not have their own transport, but it can be walked as well. There is no need to carry any camping equipment; scattered family kraals always provide some form of shelter for the night. Take along some food though. Any tasty addition to the staple diet is appreciated and encourages the locals to meet foreign travellers.

Should you prefer to stay on the tarred road, proceed straight along the MR16. Past Ka-Langa Trading Store, a number of self-help projects are underway. With foreign aid, the area has become a hive of agricultural activity. At St Paul's Catholic Mission and Primary School, basic accommodation is sometimes available. Leave a suitable donation for the upkeep of the mission. Finally, you will come to a T-junction in the road. A large signboard indicates the way left to Mhlume, Manzini and Lomahasha. To the right, is the road to Siteki and the Mozambique border.

Turning off onto the D4, the excitement for travellers starts. Visitors will now be on a good gravel road, going through an area that is still mostly unfenced bush. The previously open views become hemmed in by acacias and tall grass. It feels as though you are travelling through a quiet corridor of vegetation. Quiet only until your ears become tuned to the sounds of the wilderness. Unexpectedly, a shop looms into view; Sizanani Store. There are few customers and the owner will go to great lengths to help you. Although he has no fridge, he manages to somehow keep his drinks ice-cold and plentiful. Once past the store, you will find yourself in tribal lands. Kraals can occasionally be seen deep in the bush.

To spend an evening at one of these family kraals is surely the best way of getting to know the Swazi. Gone are the influences of modernisation. Huts are built from an inner wall of mud, followed by a lattice of sticks, then stones and finally another outer covering of mud. Don't expect a bed. You will be given a piece of earthen floor to curl up on.

When you continue driving, be careful of the crazed chickens that dash across the road at the approach of any motor vehicle. Cattle too enjoy making use of the road, and will lie in front of a vehicle, unwilling to move. Visitors who have been to India will find an amusing similarity to the sacred cows of that country.

Fever tree forests edge onto the road until the concrete causeway over the Mtindzekwa river. On either side of this usually dry river are glades of trees and secluded camping spots. Find the closest village or kraal and ask for permission to camp from the chief or headman.

About 14 km west from the turn-off on the MR16 is a fork in the gravel road. Take the right branch, but watch out for the tortoises that occasionally cross this road. Another 2 km from the Y-junction is a railway crossing. Proceed over the railway line and turn right onto the road that parallels the tracks. Follow the gravel road alongside the railway tracks. Several empty villages and kraals lie in the bush a few metres from the road.

By the time the deserted siding of Lubhuku Station appears, the road has deteriorated. Saloon cars can still cover this route however, but drive slowly and be careful of the numerous soil erosion dongas that reach to the road edges. After the station, the road curves below a railway bridge and passes isolated villages. The villagers are friendly and intrigued as to what travellers are doing here, so far from hotels and tarred roads. Further north, the road crosses back over the railway line. Ignore the road disappearing to the right, and turn left. Grotesque electricity pylons deface the landscape, carrying power to the towns and urban centres, while leaving the local villages dependent on candles and paraffin.

After the well-tended maize fields, the road once again swings back across the railway tracks. Take the right turn and continue along the road that fords several little streams, until reaching a Y-junction. From here, the bush becomes sparse and offers uncluttered landscapes. Follow the right fork in the road, just beyond the walled-in village on the right. Finally, the road skirts water reservoirs and exits at Mpaka Shopping Centre.

Foreigners seldom appear out of the bush, and you are certain to be greeted with some amazement by the numerous street vendors near Mpaka station. Buses leave from here for Siteki, Lomahasha and Manzini. It can be difficult getting a lift from Mpaka station during the week, but Sundays are easier. Many of the men who have returned home for the weekend are going back to work in the cities or South Africa, and lifts become frequent, free and fast.

The entrance to Emaswati Colliery (Swaziland Collieries) is 4 km west of Mpaka station, on the left. Emaswati colliery is Swaziland's only coal mine, but recently, a number of exploration and prospecting rights have been granted. Unofficial visits to the mine are frowned upon. Tours must be arranged with the mine management. These should be made at least three weeks before arrival. Write to the Public Relations Officer, Emaswati Coal, Post Office Siteki, Siteki, Swaziland. Tel. (09268) 34424. Guided trips are provided for visitors, which even include a visit to the coalface.

Nearby is an RSP (police) post, Khoukhona (Mr Chips) and the Tio Ze Restaurant. You will not find a maître d'hôtel here, nor tablecloths. However, the hot maize porridge with butter, thick beef stew and a jug of cereal beer are unrivalled in this hill and bush area.

The tarred road rises onto the northern edge of the Mbutini hills. Vegetation becomes thick again and there are numerous idyllic picnic sites on the summits of the passes. Close to the highest point of the trip, where you enter the province of Manzini, is a bus and taxi stop. There are splendid views into the eastern lowlands and valleys of the west. All buses stop for passengers at this lonely shelter. Many of the men wear cotton skirts with a shoulder wrap in the same design. Carrying their traditional weapons, they look out of place around a motor vehicle. Women carry children and wear minimal clothing. Their luggage is a jumble: plastic tubs hold food and children, boxes contain the odd chicken or bottles of alcohol. Plastic bags carry clothing, blankets wrap babies and also make for a soft cushion on the buses. Occasionally a collared goat will join the ride, and even less frequently someone will arrive with a battered suitcase.

From the hills, it is a gentle descent to the hamlet of Ngogola. Ngogola lies at the junction of the tarred Manzini-Siteki road and a gravel road heading south, alongside the turbulent Mzimphofu river. Here, visitors can buy intricately woven grass baskets, copper bangles and fruit at prices well below that demanded in Mbabane and Manzini. A fuel garage is open 24 hours, and Ngogola Workshop is capable of repairing minor breakdowns and punctures.

Noticeable changes will begin to appear west from the Mpisi Centre. Modern block housing replaces traditional huts and there is an increase in population. Natural bush is replaced with intensive crop cultivation, and the joyous spontaneity of the eastern Swazi retreats behind long trousers, ghetto-blasters and "dude" sunglasses.

At the turn-off for Luve is Mafutseni market where you can browse through a fair selection of handicrafts, grasswork and local clothing. There is a Caltex fuel garage at Mafutseni, and behind the handicraft shop, one of Africa's intriguing puncture repair shops. With frequent breaks for discussions and asking of questions, your whole repair operation becomes time consuming. It is however cheap, though you may like to have the job checked in Mbabane.

A small but busy bus stop is in front of the street vendors, who are a mine of information about the bus schedule. Hitching from Mafutseni can be done from the bus stop. This settlement also provides access to the tarred road which goes north as far as Mliba, where it becomes gravel to the Mananga border with South Africa.

Continuing west from Mafutseni, travellers will pass the Hotel Empandzeni and Imphandze Restaurant. Several visitors have received poor treatment at this hotel, and the apathy of the staff is clear. Manzini is a mere 14 km away, and travellers should rather find accommodation there. If you have no option but to stay at the hotel, you will be accommodated in one of 10 rooms at what is classed as a high tariff establishment. Two bars serve the predominantly travelling-salesmen guests. A dining room is available, but the food is expensive and not of good quality.

About 1 km west of the hotel, is the Ekululameni St Joseph's Mission. Education for disabled adults is provided at St Joseph's. Weaving, grasswork, tapestry and carpentry are carried out by the blind, crippled and retarded. There is a showroom that tourists should visit. The quality of work is remarkable, prices are low and whatever you pay is immediately ploughed back into maintaining and advancing the training.

J.J. Joinery, which designs, carves and builds kitchen units, is at the entrance to the road junction village of Helehele. A fuel garage, farm butchery and Helehele Store nestle close to one another. Close by is the Helehele Rest Camp. The main advantage of the rest camp is the uninterrupted views of valleys, rivers, distant mountains and forests. Rather just stop to enjoy the view instead of sleeping over.

From Helehele there is a gradual climb to the cooler climate of Manzini. Manzini is at the end of the central route. Known as the hub of the nation, Manzini is a town with an incredible convergence of roads. Most travellers usually keep going, north-west to Mbabane and to Ngwenya border post, south to Nhlangano and the Mahamba border or to one of the other 11 border posts (excluding Matsapha International Airport).

9 NORTHERN ROUTE

From Ngwenya Gate – Motshane – Pigg's Peak – Ngonini – Balegane – Tshaneni – Simunye – Lonhlupheko – Siteki – Mafutseni – Croydon – Pigg's Peak
Distance: about 460 km

FROM NGWENYA GATE

Crossing from the border post at Oshoek in South Africa to the modern and attractive building at Ngwenya is the first indication that modernisation has arrived in Swaziland. For first-timers to Swaziland, there is a tourist information computer available at the Ngwenya border. The Customs and Immigration staff are efficient and helpful. As at other Swazi border posts, have your own pen for filling in the Entry/Departure Card. Visitors using their own transport should remember that they will not be allowed to enter the country without first having obtained a Swaziland Government Road Fund ticket. The Road Fund ticket is available from the counter behind the passport-control desk.

Once through the border formalities, visitors immediately plunge into a settlement that survives on tourism. There are numerous curio stalls, selling everything from T-shirts and grass baskets to pineapples and effigies. Wait until you are further into Swaziland before buying curios, unless of course you have forgotten something and stop here on the way out.

Several buses wait in the open area in front of the stalls. Travellers using public transport will find buses to most destinations from here. Hitchhiking from here is a pleasure. With the large amount of traffic using this border post, you should not have to wait longer than 10 minutes for a lift.

Leaving the border post area, visitors travel along a tarred road past numerous shops and roadside stalls. Of particular interest, and certainly worth a visit, is Ngwenya Glass factory. This is about 5 km from the border on the left side of the road going towards Mbabane.

Allegedly named after the crocodile-shaped mountain to the northwest (it takes quite a bit of imagination or cereal brew to see this shape), the factory offers a wide selection of glass crafts. In addition to the

Swaziland Northern Route

MOZAMBIQUE

SOUTH
AFRICA

Namamcha

Lomahasha

Border Gate

Mhlumeni

Simunye

Siteki

Lonhlopheko

HLANE
GAME RESERVE

Hlane

Lukhula

Mhlume

Mpaka stn

Tshaneni

Mananga

Buckham

Miliba

Ngolola

MANTASA
HLOYANA

Jeppe's Reef

Matsamo

Balegane

Croydon

Luve

Mafutseni

Hhohho

Rocklands

NYONGANE
884

*PHONJWANE
HILLS*

Komati

MUCCUCENE RANGE

Pigg's Peak

Ndzingeni

EMLEMBE
1863m

Bulembu

MALOLOTJA
NATURE RESERVE

Enkhaba

Forbes Reef

Motshane

Mbabane

*MDZIMBA
1 494*

Ezulwini

Josefsdal

Ngwenya

MLILWANE
WILDLIFE SANCTUARY

Lobamba

Oshoek

Lundzi

Mhlambanyatsi

Waverley

goods on sale, visitors can watch the glass blowers at work. Delighted at being watched, they will even make you a particular shape if asked. Prices are high – credit cards are accepted – but the craftsmanship must rate as the highest in Africa. Recycled glass is mostly used. A percentage of profits is donated to Save the Rhino Fund. Open daily between 9h00 and 16h00, it is usually busy with tourists. Inquiries can be made by either writing or phoning.

Address: Ngwenya Glass, P.O. Box 45, Motshane, Swaziland.
Telephone: (09268) 24053/44157.

Near Ngwenya Glass is Endlotane Studios. Here, visitors can choose from an interesting collection of tapestries. The entire process of producing these works can be seen, including the application of the validation slip indicating Phumalanga authenticity. It is fascinating to watch the women at work. They are used to tourists and speak good English.

Just 8 km east of the Oshoek border, travellers arrive at the scattered settlement of Motshane. Ndumo Handicraft Centre, on the right, is a must. Not many tourists stop here but those visitors who do, are warmly received. From soapstone carvings to grass baskets, there is something for even the most fastidious of curio hunters. The women are cheerful and friendly, justly proud of their work, and drive hard but good-natured bargains. If you arrive at lunch time, visitors are certain to be invited to share a meal with some of them. This is an opportunity not to be missed; especially if it is your first visit to this beautiful country.

A few metres east of the handicraft centre, are signs indicating the way left to Pigg's Peak Hotel and Casino. To follow the northern route, turn left at Moyakazi Grocery and Motshane Grocery to reach the King Mswati II Highway. This highway is not to be confused with highways as found in Europe or the USA. It is, however, well tarred and maintained. Hitchhikers should walk a little way onto this road and wait at the pull-off area about 100 m from the corner.

At Hawane Stables visitors can hire a horse and guide for an hour. No previous experience is necessary. This is a pleasant way to explore the tiny Hawane Nature Reserve and dam across the road. Camping is available at Hawane Nature Reserve, as are fully equipped self-catering chalets. Reservations are seldom necessary, but can be made prior to arrival. Falling into the medium tariff category, Hawane Nature Reserve is empty and not of any real interest.

Address: Hawane Nature Reserve, P.O. Box 225, Mbabane, Swaziland.
Telephone: (09268) 44522, fax 42485

Further north from Hawane, across the Ngungwane river, visitors will find Timbuti Farm and Vegetables, plus a small handicraft market. Vegetarian visitors to Swaziland would do well to stop and buy some of the delicious vegetables and fruit available at this produce stall.

Large numbers of buses and minibus taxis ply this route up to Pigg's Peak, and budget travellers will have no problem catching a bus. Be sure to ask whether your lift expects payment for the ride. Visitors with their own transport need to be cautious when driving this road at night; stray cattle, overloaded buses and demented drivers can make the trip a nightmare. Try and do all your travelling in Swaziland during daylight hours.

Cold, fresh milk can sometimes be bought from the Hawane Dairy Project. Take along your own bottle and get there after 7h30 or 16h00.

Travelling north, you may notice the effects of landslides on the hills to the west. With high rainfall and monoculture practices, hillsides regularly wash away during summer storms. To make matters worse, the deforestation in this area is shocking. Hectares of rare indigenous forest are casually stripped away for agriculture. In time, the effects of this will be felt as the land becomes unfertile and production drops. Along many of the river courses, severe erosion has already slashed irreversible dongas. Much of the countryside travellers now pass through is intensively cultivated with cereal crops. On the higher hills, conifers have been planted in their thousands.

Over the Mbuluzi river, the destructive practices of modern agriculture are replaced by the gentle beauty of natural fields. Full of wildflowers on a mantle of green grass, the valleys and hills are guarded by barbed wire fences, which skirt clumps of black wattle. Along the road, vendors sell piles of firewood which they stack between upright poles. Cheap and fragrant, the wood is of little use even to campers – no open wood fires are allowed in any of the reserves of Swaziland.

At the village of Forbes Reef, you will find a Swiss chalet-style store. A guide to the abandoned Forbes Reef gold mine can be arranged here. For an official guide, you will have to pay someone from the National Trust at Malolotja Nature Reserve, about 8 km to the north. No accommodation is available at Forbes Reef itself, but if you speak to the assistant at Forbes Reef Store, you will be shown the crumbling ruins of the original Forbes Reef settlement – which was built in the late 1800s, at the time of the gold rush. Sleeping among these ruins is an eerie experience.

The tarred highway again crosses the meandering Mbuluzi river, and continues past modern houses, Forbes Reef Primary School and brightly painted villages. Traditional building materials are replaced by dazzling tin roofs and cement block walls. Past the entrance to Malolotja Environmental Education Centre is a proliferation of roadside soapstone carvers. These diligent, joint-smoking sculptors create exquisite pieces of work. They are expensive, but bargaining is accepted procedure. Be reasonable though; a great deal of work and creativity goes into each item; quibbling over a few Emalangeni is rather harsh.

About 19 km from Motshane, visitors will find the entrance to Swaziland's largest nature reserve, under the jurisdiction of the National Trust Commission.

Malolotja Nature Reserve: Medium to high tariff

Considered by many to be the country's most spectacular reserve, Malolotja encompasses two of the highest mountains and Swaziland's highest waterfall. Ngwenya peak, at 1 831 m, is also the source of the Mbuluzi river, while Silotwana at 1 681 m is near Malolotja Falls, which tumble almost 95 m before entering the Komati river system via the Malolotja river.

Situated in the highland region of Swaziland, visitors should be prepared for mist, rain and low temperatures. Malolotja's major attraction is hiking. To this end, there are trails and excursions for all grades of hikers and walkers. Game drives can also be arranged with the wardens, as can a guided tour to the oldest mine in the world. Estimated as having started as early as 41 000 BC, early man mined both specularite and haematite here. A visit to the mine should not be missed. The walking trail takes visitors through fragrant meadows filled with a bewildering variety of plant species. There are excellent opportunities for seeing blesbok, impala, wildebeest and the secretive oribi. Due to the logistics involved in this hike, prior reservations must be made. Although 24 hours ahead is suggested, it is better to book a few weeks earlier.

There are almost 200 km of well marked hiking trails. Overnight camps have been erected. Hikers should purchase a topographical map of the reserve from the main office. Permits are needed for overnight hikes and you will have to carry all your food, clothing and cooking requirements. Some prior knowledge of the outdoors is needed in this area of sudden mists and storms. For the inexperienced, there are day walks.

Less energetic visitors can always try their hand at trout-fishing in the dams. Rods and flies can be hired from the office, and a permit

obtained there. Bird-watching is another attraction. With over 250 species identified in the reserve, it is a veritable feast for amateur and
professional ornithologists. Blue swallows arrive each year, and a colony
of rare bald ibis can be seen along the arduous walk to the Malolotja
Falls. Warthog, baboon, otters and, for the very fortunate, leopard, can
be viewed on one of the guided game drives.

Accommodation is provided in five self-catering log cabins with place
for at least six people in each. Guests need to bring their own food and
drink. A small shop sells basic supplies but at inflated prices. Camping
is by far the most scenic and adventurous way of staying at the reserve.
Set on the side of a hill, each pitch is walled with its own braai area
and clump of bushes. Privacy is a prime asset, and this, coupled with
spectacular views, should make camping a definite consideration. Ablution facilities are adequate, but late arrivals can expect darkness and
cold showers. Reservations are necessary for Malolotja Nature Reserve.
These should be made at least 30 days in advance and for the festive
season, at least three months ahead.

Tariffs are high at Malolotja. There are payments for entry, car, camping or log cabin, a backpacking fee and perhaps a fishing permit. With
this array of charges it is easy to see why many budget travellers prefer
staying at the privately owned, yet cheaper, Big Game Parks of
Swaziland.

Address: The Senior Warden, Malolotja Nature Reserve, P.O. Box
             1797, Mbabane, Swaziland.
Telephone: (09268) 43060
or through Central Reservations:
Address: P.O. Box 100, Lobamba, Swaziland.
Telephone: (09268) 61178, fax 61875.

To continue on the northern route, turn left out of the Malolotja main
gate, across from Nkaba Grocery. The land is intensively cultivated as
the road descends to Bhungane Cash Store. Beyond the store, past the
wattle trees, are the stock-pens and plunge dip for the region.

Past the dipping site, travellers cross the Lubayane river and commence a series of steep gradients for about 11 km. Huts cluster together
alongside cultivated plots and curio stalls hug the road verge. Numerous
buses also use this road. If a bus passenger, avoid sitting on the left
side if travelling up to Pigg's Peak. Sheer drops and rivers will test
even the most fearless of visitors.

The road, however, is in excellent condition and driving is a pleasure. Never travel too close to a bus along this road. Debris is regularly thrown out of bus windows and can cause severe damage to vehicles close behind. On the highest section of the road, travellers will pass a little mud hut on the left with wood and soapstone carvings for sale. The sculptor loves classical music and plays Beethoven and Brahms on a battered cassette player. His carvings are especially good; particularly the Swazi busts and elephants. Visitors can watch as the man carves and whittles, with the completed image in his mind his only guide.

Contour and terrace cultivation pock the hills all the way to the heavily populated area around Malawti Grocery and Restaurant. Do not be fooled by the title, restaurant. Some food is indeed available, but the staple diet is canned beer. Seemingly filled entirely by ancient warriors carrying traditional weapons, the restaurant is a cool haven from the hot winds which blow up the valleys. Foreigners stopping here are uncommon, and the talkative octogenarians will enjoy giving you their view of Swazi history.

North of the grocery and restaurant, the road dips and rises along hillsides where ploughing is still done with oxen. Down in the valleys, the vegetation is thick and hints at what the district must have looked like before agriculture ripped the earth for crops. Just before the Komati river is crossed for the first time, a group of enterprising Swazi children try to profit from the tourist trail through here. Dressed in leaves, like so many pot-plants, they dance and sing each time a car appears. It is rather sad. This is not the real Swaziland and does not reveal the truth of these proud people.

Within a few kilometres, modern houses are replaced by more visually pleasing traditional mud, wood and thatch huts. Perched above deep valleys and toy villages, Othandweni General Dealer provides a good point from which to take photographs. Paths and tracks lead off in all directions from the store, and make for good walking if you want to escape the main road and get to meet the highland Swazi.

Driving along here over the weekend can be traumatic. Be wary of any pick-ups carrying passengers. With a reputation as the biggest consumers of alcohol per person in the world, be prepared for the odd passenger who gently topples off the side of these vans. They usually appear unhurt, smile and ask if you'd buy them a beer!

The forests of Peak Timbers then begin. The forests appear and darken the road. Hitchhiking along this road is excellent. Continue past the Phophonyane Lodge 25 km road sign until reaching the Swaziland

Plantation timber mill and yards. The hills around the site are green and attractive, offering good views onto the mill and its ominous smoke stack.

Beyond the mill is a short climb through the jacaranda-lined avenue into Pigg's Peak. About 3 km before reaching Pigg's Peak, travellers will pass a sign for Sedco Estate (Pine Furnishing). This is a good place for cheap and well made pine cabinets, drawers and benches. Of course, it can become a bit ludicrous trying to travel about Swaziland accompanied by a chair or set of shelves. The staff are, however, helpful and will arrange to send the items back to your home country.

A little further north, on the right, is the legendary Highland Inn.

Highland Inn: High tariff

Set alongside the King Mswati II Highway, this splendid inn is a frequent stop for business people. It is also a good starting point for visitors who are keen to walk the forests. Attention to detail has placed this inn on the list of Swaziland's top tourist accommodation. Neither ostentatious nor basic, it offers guests a cosy and comfortable ambience. Sitting on the wide veranda looking across hills and conifer forests is a perfect way to end the day. There are 18 rooms: one family room, 12 doubles and five singles. During quiet periods, single travellers are usually given a double room at single rates. While single rooms only have showers, all other rooms have bathrooms and showers. Double rooms have airconditioners, but with the cool climate, rich forest air and chilly nights, they are seldom used.

The tariff includes an enormous English breakfast, which is served in the rustic Woodcutter's Den. A variety of dishes are available, as is an extensive wine list. Although not on the menu, visitors should try the Scottish manager's special peri-peri chicken. Vegetarians may have a problem with the food listed, but if you mention this on arrival, every effort will be made to accommodate you. Light snacks and sandwiches can be ordered throughout the day. Two public bars open from 9h00.

Once night falls, a peaceful tranquillity settles over the inn as the traffic fades away. Reservations are not necessary, but for the New Year party they are. According to the staff, people travel from South Africa and Mozambique just for the festivities.

There is also a small campsite with access to washing facilities. A security guard is on duty from 19h00-7h00, but with the heavy, cold mist that often descends around the inn, he cannot be blamed for settling down somewhere warm.

Address: Highlands Inn, Post Office Box, Pigg's Peak, Swaziland.
Telephone: (09268) 71144.

On the veranda is Tintsaba Craft shop. A good selection of curios are on sale at set prices. The sisal baskets and dishes are renowned. Take a look at the chicken baskets which resemble large grass cooking pots. Books relating to Swaziland are next to a staggering array of earrings, bracelets and necklaces. T-shirts can be bought, as can items of hand-made pottery.

Leaving the Highlands Inn, proceed about 3 km north, along the main road, to the urban centre of Pigg's Peak.

PIGG'S PEAK

Named after French gold prospector, William Pigg, who in 1884 discovered a reef in this area, Pigg's Peak is a fascinating and exciting town. Well known among travellers, it is a centre where you are likely to encounter people from many countries. Surrounded by conifer forests, hill streams and pine-scented air, the town is ideally situated for hikers, pseudo-prospectors and lovers of the great outdoors. Pigg's Peak has retained much of its boom-town atmosphere in the rough bars and intriguing characters here. Unlike other urban centres, there are no distinct suburbs. Between modern double-story mansions are shanties and occasional traditional mud and thatch huts.

Information

There is no tourist office in Pigg's Peak, but you can get information from the manager of the Highland Inn or the RSP (police), at the northern end of town. If arriving from the north, stop at Pigg's Peak Hotel and Casino. Visitors can get tourist information at the front desk or, even better, from the banqueting manager who has been in the area for several years.

Pigg's Peak is laid out in a south-north grid. Travellers using the northern route will pass the post office on the left. The Swaziland Development and Savings Bank is opposite Select-A-Shoe in the main street. You can exchange travellers cheques here but few visitors do. Fuel is available from two garages; Total, on the right, as you go up through town, and BP, which is on the left, near Barclay's Bank. The offices of the Royal Swaziland Police (RSP) are on top of the hill, above the market. You can find them by locating the gravel yard used for driver training in front of the charge office.

South of the RSP (police), and across the road from the Baphalali Hospital and Clinic – where emergency treatment can be received – is the bus stop. Travellers will have to ask bus destinations on arrival. Minibus taxis are also available. Hitchhiking from Pigg's Peak requires that you walk past the turning for Bulembu at the northern side of town, or further south beyond the post office if going to Mbabane or Ngwenya border.

Same day drycleaning is available at Umbeluzi Dry Cleaners, near the sign indicating the way to Ka Solwako Fast Foods.

Things to see

There are no typical tourist attractions in Pigg's Peak. Visitors must be prepared to walk about if they are to find points of interest. Start a walk from the post office, at the southern end of the main street. Past Bajabula Trading Store, continue up the left side to Metro Hair and Body Care Salon. Across the road, in a tiny shop, is Sbongile Record Bar. Music pumps out of this niche and there is always a youthful crowd outside.

Climbing the hill, the road passes Moira's Dress Designs, in a small studio next to Ellerines Furnishers. Working without patterns or so-phisticated equipment, the women who work in this shop make the most intricate and exquisite clothing, especially children's clothes. They are friendly and will invite visitors in. Beaming at the unexpected visit, they will explain, in good English, what they are doing and will even go so far as to offer to make you something. Items that seem in demand from travellers are brightly coloured headbands, which are cheap and quick to make.

After the BP garage, where emergency vehicle repairs can be done, is the cluttered trading store named Kabozongo General Merchants and Furnishers. Their furniture is mass produced and uninteresting, but their selection of traditional Swazi cloth and attire is excellent.

The next point of interest is the Pigg's Peak market, on the right side of the road as you walk north from Test-of-Taste Takeaways. Pigg's Peak market is housed in an L-shaped building and deserves a visit. It is a fruit and vegetable market with an abundance of goods and hos-pitable vendors. Piles of fresh fruit and crisp vegetables fill every available concrete table and even the floor is used for displays. Buying anything will require patience and a sense of humour. No matter from whom you choose to buy, you will be challenged by others offering you a lower price. Instead of getting involved in what may resemble the start of war, allow the sellers to sort the matter out. Eventually one of the women will steer you to her counter and a purchase can be made.

North of the fresh produce market, is the true market/bazaar area of Pigg's Peak. There are shops selling virtually everything available in Swaziland. Male visitors must try having a shave or haircut at one of the barber stalls. Basic shoe repairs can be done. Both local and western clothing are on sale.

From the hospital/clinic, walk back down the main street past the line of trees on the right. Many people sedately sit for hours here and enjoy chatting to tourists. Most speak English and have both the time and patience to teach you a few words of SiSwati.

One trip that must be made while in Pigg's Peak, is to one of the largest asbestos mines in the world, Havelock (locally referred to as Bulembu, the name of the town). Go north of the hospital entrance and turn left onto the road signposted Bulembu and Barberton. There are five daily buses in each direction. Vehicles frequently travel this route and free lifts are usual if hitchhiking

West of the small industry workshops on the left, the tarred road gives way to clay. With heavy rainfalls in the district, this will prove a challenge for many people with their own transport, particularly motorcyclists. This part of the route is unsuitable for road bikes.

Steep gradients should be tackled in low gear and at low speeds. If a bus approaches from any direction it is advisable to pull off to the side until it has passed. Speed limits are not observed here and the might of buses lends them dominance over other vehicles – with the exception of giant logging trucks for whom they move over. Mist is a common occurrence in these highland forests and travellers must be careful of the timber lorries. With their heavy loads and trailers, they have an especially difficult time in wet weather. These truck drivers, however, are courteous and will go out of their way to allow you to pass safely.

Unlike the clean and tendered forests of the Usutu Pulp Company further south, the forests of Peak Timbers are poorly kept. A lot of undergrowth clogs the spaces below trees and pruning has been neglected. Should a fire erupt in these forests, it could be fatal for the isolated villages and possibly even for Pigg's Peak.

Hiking through these hills and valleys is an interesting, if strenuous, exercise. A guide can be arranged from the Highland Inn.

Hugging steep valleys, the road emerges from the forest at abandoned asbestos workings on the right. Take a walk into the quarry. Veins of asbestos can be seen and, from the top, there is an uninterrupted view over Bulembu power station to Swaziland's highest mountain, Emlembe (1 863 m).

The farmer at red-roofed Mkhomazana farm can direct hikers to the mountain and sometimes allows travellers to use one of the old sheep or cattle sheds for the night. Although it is a good starting point for a four hour hike to the summit of Emlembe, it is suggested that you get a guide from Bulembu. Leaving from Havelock will reduce the walk by at least one hour, as you will already be at the foot of the mountain in town.

From the quarry, the road drops steeply until reaching the entrance to Bulembu Power Station. Set deep in the forests on the edge of the Phophonyane river, this power station is mainly coal fired. Ash and waste are piled in wide drifts around the site and already the effects can be seen in the discoloured water and stunted growth. Progress has demanded a savage price in these valleys and many wilderness walkers are disappointed by the absence of indigenous flora and fauna. A tour can be arranged through the hissing and steaming power station. Turn right at the bridge entrance, and go down to the offices.

Hikers are welcome to leave their vehicles here should they wish to explore the surrounding forests, hills and valleys. Guides up Emlembe can be found by asking at any of the villages. To locate the remaining indigenous vegetation, tramp into the gulleys of the mountain where natural growth has survived and hidden, forgotten mine entrances preserve the mystery of these hills.

Proceeding further south-west, visitors pass along an avenue of tall, white-barked gum trees. The road is tarred from the power station. Keep to the 60 km/h limit: this final section of road to Havelock is frequently patrolled by the local RSP traffic officers.

About 20 km from Pigg's Peak, there is a security checkpoint at the sign Bulembu Asbestos Mine (Consmining). Through the checkpoint, visitors pass the golf course on the right. Entrance to the club is further west. Links are open to visitors, but it is a lot easier getting a round if you play with a local. If you want a game on this spectacular 9-hole course, speak to the Scottish manager at the Highland Inn.

Photogenic views present themselves just before you descend into the business area of the settlement. Covering the hillside to the left of the road is an extraordinarily brightly coloured housing estate. These are the homes of the mine labourers. Travellers who have been to the Faroe Islands or Greenland will see a remarkable similarity in dwellings.

Dominating the entire scene is the dust-laden asbestos mine. A fine white powder settles on everything, from trees, cars and houses, to animals, people and telephone poles. It is a unique mine though. Fascinating tours can be arranged by contacting the mine management.

Address: Havelock Asbestos Mines (Swaziland), Post Office Bulembu, Bulembu, Swaziland.

Telephone: (09268) 73244 or directly to the mine manager at 73359.

A mine-owned hospital is open to visitors. In the bottom of the cup formed by the deep valley is the post office near Riverside Store. Lutsango Handicrafts has curios that may interest visitors. Fuel is available at an Engen garage, close to the market. Behind the market, travellers will find the bus stop for buses to and from Pigg's Peak. Be certain to get there early on Friday afternoon or Saturday morning if you want a seat, as it seems most of Havelock catches these buses to Pigg's Peak.

Of particular interest is the aerial cableway, which climbs over the mountains carrying asbestos to South Africa and returns with coal for the mine and power station.

Visitors who elect to leave Swaziland via this route should note that the Bulembu border is only open from 8h00-16h00.

Leaving Pigg's Peak to continue the northern route, travellers once again take the King Mswati II Highway. Follow the road signs for Matsamo border, adhering to the 60 km/h speed limit until arriving at the stop sign, north of town. From here the speed limit is increased to 80 km/h.

Past Rocklands, and about 8 km from Pigg's Peak, visitors will see a sign indicating the way to Phophonyane Private Nature Reserve and Guest Lodge. The reserve and lodge are a considerable distance from the main road. Travellers using public transport or hitchhiking will have to get off and walk from this sign. Most vehicles using this road are going to the lodge and reserve. Drivers are friendly and you are certain of getting a lift. Turn left onto the gravel road and follow it along the edge of timber plantations. The condition of the forest road is fairly good. Upon reaching Peak Timbers guesthouse, on the right, proceed onto the bridge. From here, incredible views extend down into the valleys of northern Swaziland. On the right, after the rise from the bridge, is the entrance to Phophonyane Lodge.

The indigenous trees create a canopy as visitors descend on a steep gravel track. Drive slowly to avoid losing your vehicle's exhaust system. Natural forest creeps ever closer to the track, until travellers imagine themselves lost in some enchanted garden.

Phophonyane Lodge and Nature Reserve: High tariff

Set on the spur of a hill above the Phophonyane river, the Phophonyane Lodge and Nature Reserve is the ideal retreat for visitors in search of seclusion with first-class service.

Accommodation is provided in four cosy self-catering cottages and four safari tents. While the cottages have impressive views, the best accomodation is a furnished tent. These have a communal kitchen and washing facilities. Fitted with mosquito nets and placed within the forest, these tents are a wonderful way of getting immersed in the environment. A restaurant is available for those who do not want to cook. Meals can either be taken in the Dining Hut or eaten at your accommodation. If vegetarians inform the management prior to arrival, suitable meals will be arranged.

The lodge's greatest attraction is its catering to guests who seek peace and privacy. You do not have to meet other people or do anything. There are activities available for the more energetic keen to explore the reserve. Guided nature walks and drives can be organised to see She-langubo Gorge, interesting Nkomati Khoisan paintings, and the awesome views from Sondeza Viewpoint. One of Swaziland's many waterfalls, Phophonyane, can be seen as it tumbles down the river which flows through the reserve. The management is knowledgeable about the area and can provide visitors with detailed information concerning the flora and fauna of the 500 hectare reserve.

There are, however, a number of strange quirks concerning the administration of the lodge and reserve that visitors need to be aware of. If booking in over a weekend, you are required to book for a minimum of two nights. Entry fees must be paid each time you enter the reserve. Children are not gladly accepted, and parents are expected to keep them under strict control. Thankfully though, radios are restricted and do not shatter the tranquillity of the pristine setting. Reservations are a must and should be made at least 30 days in advance.

Address: Phophonyane Lodge and Nature Reserve, P.O. Box 199, Pigg's Peak, Swaziland.

Telephone and fax: (09268) 71310.

Returning to the tarred road, turn left onto the King Mswati II Highway. Buses regularly travel north and getting transport will be quick. Continue past Tsishingishane Motors to the entrance of Pigg's Peak Hotel and Casino on the left.

Pigg's Peak Hotel and Casino: High tariff

Located in a beautiful forest, with kilometres of thick green vegetation, the hotel and casino can be a shock if visitors have come from the remote areas of Swaziland. Through the white entrance, the road winds up past the horse stables to the security checkpoint and public car park. Stepping through tinted glass entrance doors, you could be in any top-class hotel anywhere in the world.

The staff are helpful, cordial and well trained. A vibrant atmosphere pervades the scene and visitors will soon find themselves drawn to the casino. Regular guests get preferential treatment, which induces many people to return just for the personal attention that is lavished on them. There is a tremendous social scene with disco dancing, casino facilities, including roulette and blackjack, and cabaret. There is also an airconditioned cinema complex showing x-rated movies.

Each of the 106 rooms offers views across to the Kobolondo mountains. Eight VIP rooms supply luxury accommodation. All rooms have television, telephone, radio and en suite bathroom. A duty free shop, Tekwane, is also available. With a wide variety of traditional and Western goods on sale, visitors would do well to spend a few minutes browsing. Prices are prohibitively high for most travellers, but give an indication of the diversity of handicrafts that can be found throughout Swaziland. Of particular interest is the handmade jewellery. In the entrance foyer, outside the curio shop, a local carver works. It is fascinating to watch him at work, and he is delighted to explain his craft to those who take the time to ask questions.

Conference facilities, squash, tennis and a sauna, are available to guests, as is a large swimming pool. This has a sunken bar in the water. Bars offer drinks and light meals. Full meals can be eaten in the elegant Equmeni Restaurant or the tastefully decorated Forest dining room. Most staff speak fluent English and information can also be obtained from a computerised information service at reception.

Visitors may also take part in a number of organised outdoor activities. These include horse riding, guided nature walks, putt-putt and bowls.

Pigg's Peak Hotel and Casino is luxurious and expensive. Even if you do not stay, it is worth a visit and a chance to get a good meal, before continuing your journey. Reservations are necessary and should be booked well in advance.

Address: Pigg's Peak Hotel and Casino, P.O. Box 385, Pigg's Peak,
             Swaziland.
Telephone: (09268) 71104/5, fax 71382.

Returning to the main gate, turn left back onto the highway. Falls Shopping Centre makes for an interesting visit after the First-World standards of the hotel and casino. Imbevane Restaurant serves a good selection of fast foods; especially their maize porridge and sausage. Esivivaneni Handicrafts is a small shop on the northern side of the car park. The shop attendants are soft spoken and friendly. There is no pressure to buy, but the low prices encourage purchases. On display are items of intricate grasswork, handmade pottery statues, crockery and colourful tapestries. These tapestries are also sold through Tekwane, but are at least 60 per cent less expensive if bought directly from Esivivaneni.

North from the Falls Shopping Centre, the road drops through a mixture of exotic and indigenous vegetation. When travelling in mist, slow down to 40-50 km/h, especially when rounding corners. Cattle are considered wealth to the Swazi and they will not take kindly to having a tourist injure or kill their prized possessions. As visitors get closer to the valley floor, they will notice a thickening of natural bush. The timber companies have not encroached here yet. Traditional dwellings also become more plentiful.

From the crossing over the Phophonyane river, there is a noticeable change in the temperature as the cool highlands are replaced by warm grasslands. In the Phophonyane valley, near Mishiandi Café, good hiking is possible. Follow any of the paths which crisscross the hills, passing close to kraals that offer walkers an interesting insight into the lives of these valley clans.

Across the Mgobodzi river is the Mgobodzi Agricultural Supply, Butchery and Trading Store. Surrounded by wild pawpaw trees, this is the place to get information about the surrounding district. Nearby houses, made of cement blocks, with thatch roofs and earthen floors, provide a mixture of Third and First World styles. All around the Lugungu river are frangipane trees, offset by the bright flags of a small Apostolic church made of sunburned bricks.

After passing the kraal, which is protected by a lethal barricade of acacia branches, visitors arrive at a valley, green with citrus orchards. In all directions, small trees are planted in straight rows. Tours are available during the harvest. Fruit is grown primarily for export to overseas markets. Try to visit this estate and watch the graders and pickers at work. To arrange a tour it will be necessary to ask permission from the farm manager. Follow the small sign for "Director's Corner," on the right as you drop into the valley.

About 2 km north-east is the village of **Ngonini.** As well as the Ngonini Enterprises Spar supermarket, the settlement has a Caltex fuel garage, takeaways and fruit stalls. Of particular interest are the wooden stalls between the builders supply shop and the supermarket. At these stalls you can have sewing, shoe repairs and haircuts done by smiling vendors. Behind the takeaway shop is a thatched shelter at which the locals gather on Saturday and Sunday afternoons. Next to the Spar supermarket is the post office (Eposini). The village nestles among citrus orchards, so that in season there is a wide variety of fruit available. During the off season, subtropical fruit replaces the citrus on sale. Mangoes, litchis and bananas can be bought from the vendors who sit under the trees near the fuel garage.

Hitchhiking from Ngonini is not difficult. The numerous buses that speed along the highway can also be flagged down. Walk past the fruit sellers and onto the tarred road, where you can wait for a lift. Turning right out of Ngonini, drivers pass rows of sisal along the road: these serve as natural and attractive deterrents to anyone who wants to go illegal harvesting in the fruit orchards. The Ngonini Fruit Stall, 200 m out of town, usually has a tantalising display of fruit for sale.

About 4 km from Ngonini, and across the Umjelwezi river, is a turning to the right. There are signposts for Faith's Kitchen, Balegane and Manzini. Visitors following the northern route should turn right here, onto the good gravel road. Three buses per day travel this road south: one leaves from Ngonini at 6h00, one from Matsamo border at midday, and the third from Faith's Kitchen at about 14h00. Try to catch the early bus. It is a long, hot and dusty drive to any of the distant urban centres, preferably made in the morning before it gets too hot. Minibus taxis ply this route regularly: there is at least one each hour, from about

6h00-18h00. Hitching along this road is not only difficult, but can be dangerous. There have been increasing reports of travellers getting mugged along here. Rather catch the bus or a minibus taxi from the rank opposite the Caltex garage in Ngonini.

At the Etimpisini High School sign is a mechanical repair workshop with a bright sign above the door: Luzamo Lwemaswati. Turn right here. The road doubles back alongside the King Mswati II Highway. Within 1 km of leaving the tar, travellers will find themselves in rural Swaziland. Huts are now round mud and thatch dwellings. Street vendors, who sit patiently beneath trees, sell exclusively to the locals.

Beyond Tshibe Grocery (Jibe), the hills fall away to reveal shimmering plains that stretch to the south and east in greens, browns and the bright red of flame trees. There is a single-lane bridge over the Ndlalambi river before arriving at Ndlalambi Nazarene Primary School, with its yard full of scraggly chickens and smiling children. Overnight accommodation is available in spare classrooms or by camping in the grounds of the school. Remember to leave a suitable donation if you stay. Teaching in the depths of the Swazi bush has its share of difficulties for the young women teachers who are posted here. It makes for enlightening conversation to hear what their hopes and dreams are.

Outside O.K.K. Ndlalambi Store – where fuel is occasionally available – is a mixture of bus graveyard and fruit market. No tourist trinkets are for sale in this lonely outpost, but the people are gracious and hospitable. Over the Natali river, with its severely eroded banks, is the Shewgwene Mission and Hospital. The buildings are brightly painted and modern. Although the staff are overworked, they enjoy having unexpected visitors and will take a few minutes to give you a cup of tea and a quick tour of the hospital.

Settlements crowd in close to the road from the hospital. Contours carve up small hills and the rich smell of newly turned earth is like a balm. Intensive agriculture is practised all the way past Mayiwane Store to the Nsonyama river. From the hilltops around Entokozweni Store there are magnificent views into the valleys. On weekends – particularly Saturday afternoon – men in traditional Swazi dress and with weapons, congregate around the nearby Emazulwini Store. With leopard skirts, lion's teeth around their necks and sharp spears behind cowhide shields, they present foreigners with a unique image. Few tourists come this way and you can be sure of an amicable reception should you stop.

Situated in a grove of mango trees, Emkhuzweni Health Centre (Holiness Union Mission), also offers campers basic facilities. Traditional Swazi food can be bought from Vuka General Dealer and Bar. Accommodation in villages can be found by asking at the Eyami Shopping Centre, close to the Caltex fuel garage. There is an office of the RSP (police) here, as well as a Pep clothing store and busy bottle-store.

South of this business area is a crossroads. Continue across this and over the cattle grid. On the banks of the Mpofo river, herdboys lounge around or swim in the shallows. Their stick-fighting ability is truly amazing and, if they put on an exhibition for you, you will easily see why they have stuck to carrying traditional weapons in this wilderness. From here, the road is frequently graded, which makes it easier for four-wheeled vehicles, but extremely difficult for two-wheelers.

Vegetation gets thicker again, the villagers now only cultivating the little plots immediately around their huts. At Emvangathi bus stop, street vendors sell fruit, stunted vegetables and beef stew. Woodland kingfishers abound in this area and visitors will often see the brightly coloured little birds rocking gently on the telephone and electricity lines. Proceeding south, drivers should take note of the many broken and twisted bodies of vehicles that have plunged off the gravel into dongas and ditches. During the rainy summer season, this road is treacherous and difficult. It should only be attempted in the dry winter or autumn months.

Travellers then enter a region of silence and tranquillity. There are scattered huts and kraals here, but apart from a few stores, you will be quite alone in the Swazi bush. Rocky hills creep in towards the road behind Phamakama General Dealer. By walking into these hills around Nyakatfo Woodlot, Orchard and Vegetable Project, visitors can get unobstructed views of parts of Swaziland not served by main roads. Paths link these places and you must shoulder a pack, tent and food, if you are to get to the villages in the hills.

Past Bambanani Cotton and Orchard Growers is a concrete causeway, and Ka-Tfusi bus stop. Buses are infrequent and many travellers using public transport hitch this stretch of road south. The crowd that waits in the early morning and late afternoon seem to enjoy having a tourist travelling with them. South of the roadworks camp is the Mzimnene river. Thursday is wash day, and women from the villages descend in droves to do their laundry.

About 4 km from the Mzimnene river is a T-junction. To the right is the road going to Pigg's Peak and Bulembu. Balegane, Tshaneni and

Manzini are straight on as the northern route continues. On the second part of this route, travellers will return to this junction and proceed west to Pigg's Peak again.

A low-level bridge over the Komati river follows. During the rainy season, this bridge is often under water and drivers should cross with caution. Empty stream beds are passed until reaching a Y-junction. Turn left for Tshaneni, about 38 km to the north, near the Mananga border with South Africa. At Dvokolwako there is a shop named Tihlahla Tesine National Herbs. There are countless herbs and remedies on sale. The traditional healer speaks poor English but is delighted that visitors show an interest in the tribal arts. In the same area is a butchery and Madlangemisi General Dealer, at which fuel is sometimes available.

Balegane switch yard breaks the natural scenery before travellers pass the Church of the Nazarene Balegane Clinic. Attending primarily to the needs of locals, medical treatment is also available to visitors.

The hills retreat past the clinic, and visitors find themselves on a flat brown plain. This is the site of the infamous Balegane prison farm. With a reputation for severity, the mere name causes alarm in many Swazis. There are high signs warning people: Balegane Prison Farms. Fuel is on sale at Balegane Prison Store but the shop assistants are neither friendly nor helpful, and seem suspicious of foreigners who stop here. The area around Balegane is well maintained, clean and orderly (there is obviously an abundance of free labour).

North-east of this depressing settlement, travellers will find Sikhun-yana High School. Grass is sparse, animals look gaunt and hungry, and even the few trees look stunted. Pupils at the school are not friendly and for some odd reason throw stones at passing foreigners, especially if they happen to be white. It is unlike other rural areas of Swaziland, where visitors encounter only welcomes and hospitality.

Behind Shume Café, where diesel and paraffin are available, is a quaint village set in thickly bushed hills. The villagers are eager to invite visitors into their homes, and offer a simple but filling meal.

Further east is I.Y.S.I.S. (Komati Weir). Continue along the gravel road into a region full of aloes. Traditional homes are replaced by painted square-framed houses around Mangelda Central School. A cattle-grid marks the entrance to the company owned lands of Inyoni Yami Swaziland Irrigation Scheme (I.Y.S.I.S.).

A turning to the right, on a gravel road, goes south and then west to Mliba (which is described further along the northern route). Barbed wire fences now demarcate pastures. Gates labelled with numbers close off the bush, and both huts and people disappear from the scene. About 2 km from the Mliba turn-off, is a road left to the Sand river dam. Travellers can camp at Sand river dam, but there are no facilities, bilharzia is a problem and you need to take all your own equipment and food for the duration of the stay.

Finally, visitors arrive at a circle on the MR5 tarred road. North is to the Mananga border, south to Balegane (the way you have just come), east to Tshaneni and Manzini and west for Sihhoye. Go around the circle and out the eastern side. Several warning humps cross the road before the entrance to Tshaneni.

TSHANENI

Another company owned town, Tshaneni is a replica of other agricultural company sites. It is the largest town in north-eastern Swaziland and a stop along the northern route for many visitors.

The entrance to town is proclaimed by a vertical plank with the name, Tshaneni, branded into the wood. A large sign points the way to the Impala Arms hotel. Colourful bougainvillea lines the route into town. A manicured island separates a dual carriageway. Information about Tshaneni is available either from the manager of the Impala Arms hotel or from the S.I.S. offices. Turn left at the circle into Komati Road. Another circle soon appears. Go three-quarters of the way around this circle, following the signs for the post office and bank. The post office is on the corner of Sigwaca and Lutala Roads. Near the post office is a branch of Barclay's Bank which has the habit of closing during lunch time (awkward for travellers passing through.) The headquarters of S.I.S. are on Lutala Road.

Return to Mangena Road, the entrance to Tshaneni, and turn left at the circle to reach the CBD. There is a T-junction in the middle of town. At right angles to Mangena Road is Impala Road. Directly across from the stop street is the Impala Arms hotel. A fuel garage is to the left, as is Fairways Cash and Carry, a bottle-store and Cash Build.

Impala Arms Hotel: Medium tariff

If you want accommodation in Tshaneni, then this is really the only place available. Owned by the Deputy Prime Minister, there are three categories of accommodation in a descending price range. All rooms have washing facilities en suite. A residents' lounge complete with leather sofas, television and local Swazi art provides seclusion for guests. Two bars serve the clientele. A small but exclusive boutique and curio shop is situated across from the public bar. On weekends, a vibrant disco takes place in the hall in front of the reception area.

Vegetarians are not catered for, and you will have to order boiled vegetables for your meal. The Impala Arms is more a stopover than a place where someone might spend a vacation. Reservations are not necessary as few of the rooms are ever occupied. However, should you prefer everything prepared, you can write to the manager for a booking.

Address: Impala Arms Hotel, P.O. Box 34, Tshaneni, Swaziland. Telephone: (09268) 31244, fax 31045.

There is a small clinic alongside the hotel. A fruit and vegetable market is located behind the bus stop going west up Impala Road. This bus stop and market can be difficult to find. The best landmark to look for is Asihlolisane General Dealer as you enter Impala Road.

Few long distance buses or minibus taxis leave from Tshaneni and you may find yourself having to take a number of short hops before reaching a distant destination. There are however daily buses leaving and arriving from Siteki, Mananga border post and Simunye. Three mornings per week a bus makes the journey to Manzini, while on Wednesday at 9h00 a bus takes the gravel road to Mliba. Hitchhiking from Tshaneni is not at all difficult. Many of the truck drivers enjoy company on their long and usually solitary trips across country. Ask whether a fee is expected and settle this before setting off.

Causarina trees line most of the quiet suburban roads. While not as attractive as the pine trees of the highlands, they do make the most beautiful sound when the afternoon wind blows through them. Alongside the Swaziland Library Service, across from Delcor Butchery, is the local soccer field. Matches here are subdued in comparison to those in other parts of Swaziland, but the standard of football is high.

Leaving Tshaneni, turn right outside town, across from Road Side Fruit Stall. Continue on this tarred road which winds through sugar cane fields. The Tshaneni RSP (police) have a modern building along this road. They are helpful to travellers and can give accurate directions to Mhlume Sugar Company.

On both sides of this road, sugar cane grows under high irrigation sprinklers. To supply these systems, irrigation canals have been dug along the edges of fields. This is a hot and humid part of Swaziland

and travellers may feel tempted to lie down in a canal for a quick cool off. Not only is this inadvisable due to bilharzia, but it will also incur the wrath of management should you get caught.

There are the inevitable speed humps as you enter Mhlume past the railway station. At the circle, visitors with their own transport have the choice of going to the mill, to the Shell fuel garage or Mhlume village, or continuing south-east. Most travellers go directly past Mhlume. Further on, on the right, is the route indicator showing straight for Manzini and Lomahasha, right to Mhlume Mill (which can be seen to the west) and left into the yards of Cargo Carriers. South of this sign is an elaborate board pointing the way left to Mananga Agricultural Training Centre.

From Mananga Agricultural Training Centre proceed south-east. As banana trees become prolific, travellers arrive at the Jubilee Motel. With excellent accommodation less than an hour south, at Hlane, and the more comfortable Impala Arms in Tshaneni, this motel is not recommended

South-east from the Jubilee Motel is a sign showing the way to Vuvulane farms. Next is another vast agricultural holding under the ownership of Tambankulu Estates. There is a tiny settlement comprising Tambankulu Stadium, the estates head office, Fairways Supermarket and the Hair Citi Salon.

This hamlet is protected by hundreds of carefully planted citrus trees which roll away to where nature has made her stand in the foothills. Visits can be arranged, but you should make a reservation. Write or telephone the manager at:

Tambankulu Estates, P.Bag Mhlume, Swaziland.
Telephone: (09268) 31043.

A small handicraft shop has been set up at Tambankulu Estates which is popular with visitors to this region. Prices are fixed, but the quality of workmanship is high. For specific items contact the shop directly. Tel. (09268) 38928.

East of Tambankulu Estates, the road passes through a strip of natural vegetation before arriving at a T-junction and Maphiveni village. Buses and minibus taxis from all over north-eastern Swaziland converge here. The Lomahasha border with South Africa is only about 20 km to the north. Fuel is available at Brown's Motors and Caltex garage. Travellers heading north can expect at least one military roadblock on that road. Buses going south and west can be found outside the fuel garage. Street vendors sit quietly amidst the litter, oblivious to their surroundings, intent only upon survival.

Turn right through Maphiveni and go across the Mbuluzi river, which was first crossed on the northern route near Hawane Nature Reserve and Dam, in the far west of Swaziland. On the other side of the river, travellers enter the cultivated lands of Umbuluzi Estates, which falls under the management of Tambankulu Estates. Visitors are allowed to walk through the lands unguided but should give the managers some warning by telephoning Umbuluzi Canes office, tel. (09268) 38710.

A road sign indicates south-west for Manzini or left to Mlawula Nature Reserve.

Mlawula Nature Reserve: High tariff

Spread out across lowlands and the heights of the Lebombo mountains, Mlawula is administered by the Swaziland National Trust Commission (like Malolotja in the west). Guided or independent walks can be taken through the reserve.

Covering over 18 000 hectares, the reserve is sanctuary to several rare species, including Sharpe's grysbok, mountain reedbuck and sa-mango monkeys. Plant life is also varied and no visit to the reserve is complete without a trip to see the endangered Lebombo ironwood trees. With the aid of a guide, it is also possible to find varieties of cycads that are not found anywhere else in the world. Nearly 300 bird species inhabit the reserve, including the rare African finfoot and yellowspotted nicator.

As at Malolotja, foreigners are required to pay a higher fee than locals. There are entrance fees, camping and backpacking charges, car fees and the cost of the tented camp as well.

Accommodation for self-catering visitors is provided in three tents. Cooking facilities are available, as are ablution amenities. Camping in the designated campsite is a cheaper way of staying here, with each pitch having access to washing and cooking areas. Hikers who have prudently requested the services of a guide are permitted to overnight at Ndzindza Cottage, accessible only to hikers. Reservations are strongly recommended, even for campers, particularly in the popular summer months. It is also a good idea to arrange for a guide if you plan to hike.

Address: Senior Warden, Mlawula Nature Reserve, P.O. Box 312, Simunye, Swaziland.
Telephone: (09268) 38885.

Central Reservations, P.O. Box 100, Lobamba, Swaziland.
Telephone: (09268) 61516/61178.

Turn left back onto the main road at Mlawula Restaurant and Bar. Cheap, tasty and filling meals are available at this restaurant. A dubious crowd hangs out here, but they are exuberant and friendly. Do not be surprised if a few of them are poachers.

There is a lookout tower further south-west. Stop and climb to the top of this structure. Good views extend across thousands of hectares of sugar cane to the brown bulk of the Lebombo mountains in the east. In late summer, the area is warm and pleasant with gentle afternoon breezes and whispers from the bright green sugar cane.

Visitors will no doubt notice the convoys of military vehicles that use this road. Linking Swaziland to war-ravaged Mozambique, these roads are heavily patrolled, with frequent checkpoints. Aware of this corridor for smuggling weapons, South Africa has demanded that something be done to limit the transit of guns for criminals. Observe caution when taking photographs along the eastern edges of Swaziland; several non-obvious points are considered sensitive. Rather get permission from the Station Commander at the RSP (police) in nearby Simunye.

Simunye Estates has become one of the most successful agricultural projects in Swaziland. Officially opened in 1980 by the late King Sobhuza II, it now covers almost 10 000 hectares of sugar cane. Producing record crops, such as a staggering 166 000 tonnes in 1992, Simunye Sugar Estates is the largest employer in the country. An entire town has been built by the company which trades under the name of The Royal Swaziland Sugar Corporation Limited. Tours of the facilities, estates, mill, training centre and workshops can be arranged through the Public Relations Officer.

Address: The Royal Swaziland Sugar Corporation, Simunye Sugar Estate, P.O. Box 1, Simunye, Swaziland.
Telephone: (09268) 38600, fax 52646 ext 4045.

SIMUNYE VILLAGE

Turn left into this quaint village, deep in a sea of green sugar cane fields. Immediately left is a Caltex fuel garage, Score Supermarket and A & B Motors, which specialises in mechanical and panelbeating repairs. Past the garage is a tarred road that leads towards the CBD. Take care of the speed humps.

In front of Score Supermarket and Simunye Plaza is the bus and minibus taxi depot. On Wednesday and Saturday, buses make the trip to Manzini, while from Monday to Friday there are several buses going south and then east to Siteki, or north towards Lomahasha and Mananga. Taxis cover most routes as far as Manzini or Lomahasha daily. Although more costly than buses, they are comfortable, fast and frequent.

Simunye Plaza resembles a glass fortress. Virtually all the shops face inwards onto a grubby garden. There are, however, numerous shops for a company town. At the Country Kitchen you can order from a range of both traditional and American style meals; as takeaways or eaten at the little tables.

Same day dry cleaning is offered at Umbeluzi Dry Cleaners, near the well-stocked chemist. To get your clothes back the same day they will have to be handed in before 9h00. Visitors who are planning to spend a few days in the self-catering accommodation at Hlane Game Sanctuary should stock up on fruit and vegetables from the Nondumiso Green Door fruit and vegetable shop. Neither of the two banks in the plaza, Barclay's Bank and Swaziland Development Bank, are experienced at changing travellers cheques and refuse cash advances drawn against credit cards.

Leaving Simunye Village, turn left at the Caltex fuel garage onto the main tarred road. Further south are the signs for Lusoti, RSP (police) and Swazi Sun Valley resort. Beyond these signs, vehicles cross a cattle grid into Hlane Game Sanctuary. Fences disappear on the sides of the road and drivers need to be alert for wildlife – as shown by warning road signs. For the sake of the wildlife and Swazi law, keep to the 60 km/h speed limit. Turn right at the sign for Hlane National Park.

Hlane Royal National Park: Medium tariff

Founded with wisdom and foresight by King Sobhuza II in 1967, Hlane Royal National Park remains held in trust for the Swazi nation. The son of Sobhuza, Mswati III, who now rules, continues to play an active role in the protection and patronage of this wildlife sanctuary on the edge of the majestic Lebombo mountains. Justly earning its royal title, it is one reserve that should not be missed in any tour of Swaziland.

At the electrified entrance there is a grim warning to poachers; hundreds of snares and torn items of clothing are draped over wire lines. The efficiency and capability of its staff is immediately obvious when entering Hlane. They are helpful, informative and have many stories to tell. Covering more than 70 000 hectares, this game sanctuary is home to an abundance of wildlife, including hippo, elephant, white rhino (dehorned), giraffe, zebra, impala and many others. The most exciting event is the soon to be carried out reintroduction of lions into Hlane. In SiSwati "Ngwenyama" means lion – the creature of kings, the royal animal.

Hlane boasts the largest concentration of raptors in Swaziland, and birdwatchers flock there during the spring and summer months.

Accommodation is provided for all types of visitors. Situated at a waterhole, Ndlovu Camp has a flat, spacious camping and caravan site. Full ablution facilities are available. Ostriches that wander through the camp are a delightful addition to the scene. There is a fully supplied self-catering family hut with two double rooms and a loft section. Another, smaller hut, with dormitory style accommodation of three single beds, is used mostly by budget travellers tired of camping.

For a real experience of the African wilderness, book into one of the three self-catering cottages at remote Bhubesi Camp. These electrified cottages are each hidden in their own private piece of Africa overlooking the sluggish Mbuluzana river. In the evenings, there is the euphoric feeling of being lost in the timelessness of the African bush.

Hlane is a typically African game park, with acacia trees and sun-burned savanna grasslands. There are several interesting hikes tailored to the requirements of walkers. Guides can be arranged for a small fee and will prove informative on the trail. Game drives are not conducted in the usual way. You use your own vehicle accompanied by a ranger. Visitors with their own transport can obtain a map from the main gate and go on a game drive on their own.

Even though you will need to take along all your own food for the duration of the stay, staying at Hlane is a memorable and rejuvenating experience.

Reservations are a necessity and must be done at least 60-90 days ahead. Detailed information on environmental and conservation matters can also be directed to the same address.

Address: Big Game Parks, P.O. Box 33, Mbabane, Swaziland.
Telephone: (09268) 61591/2/3, fax 61594.

or through their Central Reservations at:

Address: Big Game Parks, P.O. Box 234, Mbabane, Swaziland.
Telephone: (09268) 45006, fax 44246.

Continuing south from Hlane, follow the signs for Manzini. The turn-off to the sanctuary is the best place to start hitching from. There is the chance of getting a lift either with park visitors or from vehicles from Simunye's direction. Buses and minibus taxis frequently travel this road from central and south-eastern Swaziland to the Lomahasha border and back.

The road travels for some way through the sanctuary, the tranquillity disturbed occasionally by skittish buck that dart across the tarmac. There is a slight rise to cross the railway line, Hlane's boundary.

Travellers are immediately thrown into the man-made world of farms, crops, domestic livestock and villages. Barbed wire fences once again line the road. Valleys roll away to the south and east, revealing gaily coloured settlements and intensive contour cultivation. In some corners of these agricultural lands the bush has not yet yielded and delicately shaped fever trees sooth the eye. Birds of prey roost here and can be seen soaring hundreds of metres up in the sky.

At Maphatsindvuku Grocery, turn left for the mountain town of Siteki, about 14 km to the east. Go past the Tutta Italia signboard and the water reservoir, to where extensive views extend over the southern valleys. Khutsala Poultry Project, funded by the EEC, is the pilot enterprise for this region of Swaziland. Nearly 5 km from the turn-off is a Y-junction. The right turn goes south towards Big Bend. Turning left for Siteki, the road begins to climb into the foothills of Swaziland's eastern border, the Lebombo mountains.

From the acacias and savanna of the lowlands, the vegetation now becomes lush and thick, with an olive green colour. The trees are mostly indigenous. They pack the ravines and hill gulleys offering walkers excellent routes. At the start of the steepest part of the road is a foot-and-mouth control barrier and fence. Everyone is required to stop and be inspected here; both going up and coming down. Look back onto the flat lowlands of Swaziland. Heat rises from these plains, throwing up a veil of dust that makes for stunning sunsets.

From the summit of this hill, virtually the whole of Swaziland can be seen. Visitors can see west to the Kobolondo and Ntababomvu mountains; north to the glittering Sand river dam; south over Nyetane dam and towards the Mhlosheni range border area and east to the rocky hills of the high Lebombo mountains that border Mozambique.

Going on towards Siteki, travellers pass Sizabantu Motor Garage, Ekungobeni Trading Store and Swaziland's National Fire and Emergency station. Camping in these hills is not safe near the populated areas, but sometimes lodgings can be found by enquiring at the Mzilikazi Takeaways near the Caltex fuel garage and Majina Trading Store.

Exotic trees replace natural growth. Squatter shacks and both modern and traditional housing compete for valuable hill space. Blessed with a high rainfall and temperate climate, plant life grows in the strangest of places. Green grass on thatch roofs, ferns from gutter pipes, and wildflowers in every available ditch and drain. The Swaziland Nazarene Bible College and Library is just outside town. Basic accommodation can be had if room is available. No fee is asked, even if you get invited to share in a filling meal, but leave a suitable donation. A Red Cross clinic is across the road from the bible college, where first aid is available if someone is on duty. An explosion of housing development among groves of conifers marks the entrance to Siteki.

SITEKI

Huddled on a hillside, and surrounded by tall trees, Siteki is one of Swaziland's most attractive centres. Meaning "marriage site", Siteki is one of the highest towns in the country. Swaziland's oldest colonial centre has an air of history still clinging to many of the old buildings.

Arriving in Siteki, travellers will pass the Stegi Hotel on the left. Across from the hotel is a Shell fuel garage and Carway Motors, where basic repairs and efficient panelbeating can be done. East of the mechanical workshop, turn right into the main road and CBD of Siteki.

The Wild East Restaurant, on the right, has an à la carte menu, takeaways and a delicious Sunday brunch from 11h00-15h00. The restaurant is popular with travellers and you are as likely to meet a visitor from Copenhagen as someone from Mbabane. At the Home Restaurant, there is a wide selection of American and Swazi style meals for sale.

To meet the locals, visit the Entokozweni Beer Hall. Turn right at Select-A-Shoe and follow the signs and noise to the hall. There is always a crowd and it is a good place to ask where cheap lodgings can be found. The patrons are affable and helpful.

The bus and taxi rank is across from Evukuzenzele Multi Market. A colourful and vibrant market is located behind the bus stop. Buses and taxis serve most of Swaziland from here. Even trans-border buses for South Africa's major cities can be found at the Siteki bus depot. It may seem to be total chaos on arrival, but within a few minutes most travellers will have found where to catch the correct bus. Saloon car taxis line up under the trees, along the main road. These taxis make the shorter local trips.

There are actually two markets. One is the official fruit and vegetable market. Fresh vegetables and fruit are laid out on concrete tables for inspection while, at the northern end of the complex, is a small walled section for cooked food sales. The women in the produce market are vocal and not averse to using a little physical force on vacillating customers.

Visitors can buy eggs from the Egg Pilot Project (Khutsala Poultry Co-op). Check the age of these eggs as salmonella might be a problem. Avoid buying the eggs on display in the hot sun; ask for those kept under the counter.

Clothing is laid out in colourful piles on blankets behind the market. There is a wide selection of Western clothing, all at highly negotiable prices. For curio hunters, Swaziland T-shirts can be found for sale from the young women who sit in front of the public toilets. Walk up past the clothes sellers to the row of small stalls to the right of the fresh produce market. Of particular interest is the last shop in the row, Ntenteni Muti Manufacturers. This is a traditional medicine shop. A vast array of intriguing and fascinating objects are hung on wire lines.

Across the road, and to the right of the bus and taxi depot, is Swaziland Development and Savings Bank. It is almost impossible to get anything done at this bank if you are not from Swaziland. Travellers cheques are unheard of and cash currency exchanges are refused.

Turn left at the bank, and go up the road, turning right at Emcozini Grocery and Restaurant. East of this area is the Weights and Measures office, on the left of the tarred road, and the Royal Swaziland Police Lubombo Regional Headquarters.

The post office is beneath towering aerials in front of the Government Services Building. Next to the post office is the charge office of the Siteki RSP (police). Service is quick and efficient at the Siteki post office. It is one of the few post offices in Swaziland where it is possible to receive poste restante post. The postmaster will keep letters for three weeks before returning them to the main post office in Mbabane. Information on medical treatment can be obtained in the building next to the post office. There are inevitably long queues with people waiting for attention, but the process can be accelerated by going directly to the Superintendent's office for assistance.

By going down past the RSP (police), and then turning right, visitors will find an old Anglican church set in a neglected but captivating garden. No-one is quite sure when the church was built.

Newspapers and magazines can be found on sale at Webster's Books, across the road from Ramao's General Electrical and Refrigeration. Publications containing information on other parts of Swaziland can also be obtained here.

There are attractive walks in the hills and valleys. Be careful however; it is a sensitive border area with Mozambique a few kilometres east. Get permission to explore and camp here. This can be obtained by speaking to the Chief of Police at the Lubombo Regional Headquarters. He is a helpful man, who will go out of his way to offer advice to campers and assist them with a letter in SiSwati, for chiefs through whose land you might walk.

Accommodation for tourists is limited in Siteki.

Stegi Hotel: High to medium tariff

The air of faded grandeur is immediately obvious upon entering this small hotel. One of the oldest hotels in Swaziland, the atmosphere of neglect and decay detract from what could be one of the most colonial and imaginative places to stay in the kingdom.

At reception, expect rude and often curt service. The manager is seldom available to answer guests' questions and the staff will do little to help visitors. Eight rooms with bathrooms are available, as is a large dining room and residents lounge, festooned with contemporary African art. A small menu caters to limited tastes and offers nothing for vegetarian guests. The hotel is however close to town and eating establishments where cheaper meals are available. It provides accommodation mostly to travelling businessmen – hitchhikers can usually arrange lifts from the hotel. Reservations are not necessary.

Address: Stegi Hotel, P.O. Box 33, Siteki, Swaziland.
Telephone: (09268) 34126.

Most travellers are reluctant to leave the beauty and tranquillity of Siteki, but sooner or later the trip back to the hot plains must be made. Return west, back past the foot-and-mouth boom; where your packs, vehicles and luggage will be rechecked, this time more thoroughly. Then there is a descent onto the savanna of the lowveld. Continue past Siteki Nazarene Primary School. From Matsetsa Roadside Store, follow the route indicators for Manzini.

There is little to encourage visitors to stop at Mpaka, and unless you have stamped clearance, the security guards will not allow people into Mpaka Railway Village.

Details of the route from Mpaka Station to Mafutseni can be found in the chapter on the central route.

To continue on the northern route, turn right at the Caltex fuel garage and Mafutseni Trading Store about 28 km west of Mpaka. Signboards point north to Luve and Mliba, along a well maintained tar road. Small, intensively cultivated and irrigated plots line the road from the turn-off until the entrance to Mafutseni Ranch.

In summer, this stretch is scorchingly hot. The best time to drive to Mliba is early morning, between about 6h00 and 8h00. Crossing the Mbuluzana river, visitors are likely to encounter one of the numerous buses that serve the region from Mliba to Mafutseni and Manzini. These vehicles stop to the north of the crossing, to fill their radiators with water, before the climb to Mafutseni.

About 17 km from Mafutseni is the left turn for the village of Luve, where fuel is available. Luve is a dusty and inhospitable grassland settlement. Most of the men work in South Africa. Villagers left behind are suspicious of foreigners and show no signs of friendliness.

Stay on the tarred road going north-east. After passing traditional Swazi dwellings, travellers arrive at the Umbuluzi Barracks and Training Battalion. This is one place where neither visitors nor photographers are welcome.

Visitors who do not mind some strenuous walking, should look for the relay station on top of the hill to the north of the camp. There are scenic panoramas from the summit of this hill; the sweat and effort will be well worth it once you arrive at the summit. From Emthonjeni Cash Store, follow the row of tall poles running up the hill to the relay station. It should take about an hour to reach the top. You will be able to see the camp, rolling plains and shallow valleys with mud and thatch villages. To the north-east, Mnjoli dam glitters under the Swazi sun.

A gravel road turns to the left 1 km from Mliba. This is the road for Balegane. Those using public transport should get off here and walk a little way onto the gravel road. Only two buses per day serve this stretch of road and most people start hitchhiking. Traffic is scarce, but you may be assured of a lift on the first vehicle that comes along.

Any semblance to Western houses rapidly vanishes and travellers will once again be in tribal Swaziland. The continuation of traditional kraals stops at Croydon. It was Bill Buckham, adventurer, explorer and traveller, who settled in this area and named the locale after his home suburb in London. Sitting in the immensity of the bush, Croydon boasts Croydon Highway Motors, Endvulo General Dealer, the ubiquitous bottle-store and Croydon Wine and Malt Bar.

Thick bush encroaches on the road until an estate agent's sign at Buzzby Services. Across the road is Croydon Scrapyard, which is full of relics which elsewhere would be snapped up by ardent collectors.

A European Economic Community bridge, known as Dvokolwako Bailey Bridge, has been built across the Black Mbuluzi river. During summer rains, the single-lane bridge is often flooded. Extreme care needs to be taken when fording the flow. Allow the vehicle on the bridge to get off completely before mounting the structure.

Agricultural projects and rural education centres blossom along the road north. Much foreign aid pours annually into Swaziland with a large portion of it being ploughed into agriculture and education.

Outside Mfelankhono General Dealer and Butchery are street vendors who sell hot, buttered porridge and goat stew. Chicken curry is also available.

Proceed on this gravel road north until reaching Mnyokanyoka Grocery, where fuel is sometimes obtainable. There is a Y-junction here that visitors on the northern route will have passed on the drive to Tshaneni. Keep left, past Madlangempisi General Dealer, and take the road to Pigg's Peak. Outside Tihlahla Tesive Traditional Healer is a depot for buses coming and going west to Pigg's Peak, north to Matsamo border, east to Tshaneni and south to Manzini. This is also a good spot from which to hitchhike, as many drivers stop for quick liquid refreshment from the street vendors.

Past Mzaceni General Dealer, you need to slow down when approaching the blind corner. This corner becomes wickedly slippery after the slightest rain. Another low level single-lane bridge crosses the wide Komati river, where women can be found scrubbing clothes and blankets on Saturday mornings.

From the Komati river, the road climbs through a pass in the rocky hills, before dropping to a valley covered in wildflowers. Red, yellow and orange blossoms colour many of the indigenous trees during summer and autumn. About 22 km from Croydon, the road reaches a Y-junction. A route board indicates left to Pigg's Peak and Bulembu and straight on for Matsamo border.

Turning left, travellers commence the first of many long and winding climbs towards the western highlands. This is uncharted hiking country, but it is advisable to get permission first. This can be obtained from the Superintendent in the offices to the right of the turn for Pigg's Peak and Bulembu. Camping is also possible in this maze of hills, but you will need to take along your own food, camping and cooking equipment. Habitation is sparse, but the locals will happily provide you with fresh milk and a few eggs. Money is not expected and bartering is preferable.

Continuing west, the vegetation becomes more dense, crowding in close to the road. A sign for Balegane Ranch lies about 4 km from the turn-off in a wilderness of trees and grassland. At Shelton Memorial church, the road once again rises until crossing the D84 road, which turns right for the settlement of Jacks, 23 km to the north. Once past the bus stop at Sibetsamoya Store, the route enters a populated area.

About 200 m north from the corner is Bulandzeni Grocery, where fuel is available. A sign for St Peregrine's Mission is across from the turning, in front of Emthantazweni General Dealer. Accommodation suitable for travellers can be found at the mission. It is suggested that prior enquiries be made. Contact the Father. Address: St Peregrine's Mission, P.O. Box 107, Pigg's Peak, Swaziland.

Climbing west from the mission, the road struggles up to high hills. Villages nestle in forested gulleys, while guava trees proliferate on the rounded hilltops. At the steepest point in the road, visitors should stop and look back the way they have travelled. There are spectacular views over lowland valleys, rivers and plains.

Descending from this mountain pass, the alpine setting is enhanced by the appearance of evergreen trees and high meadows of purple, yellow, white and blue wild flowers. West of the Enzingeni Nazarene mission, clinic and school, indigenous flora is replaced by the exotic gum and conifer trees of Peak Forests. An avenue of jacaranda trees leads to the sign Mondi Forests: Peak.

Inqaba Ye Mswati café – which serves iced cold-drinks and steaming vegetable stew – marks the start of the 40 km/h speed limit to Pigg's Peak Timber Mill. Across the narrow bridge, visitors will find themselves back on a tarred road past the entrance to the mill.

The road continues west through Ekuthuleni settlement, surrounded with shadowy woodlands and deep valleys. The road here is blasted out of steep hillsides. There is an increase in the speed limit, to 60 km/h, as far as the T-junction. At the junction, travellers enter King Mswati II Highway and the end of the northern route.

From here, visitors have three options. West is the scenic and challenging gravel road via Pigg's Peak to the mountain border post at Bulembu. North the tarred road goes nearly 40 km to Matsamo border, while south it returns along the initial part of the northern route, via Pigg's Peak, Forbes Reef and Motshane. From Motshane, the choice is either west out through Ngwenya border post, or south-east to Mbabane and the Ezulwini valley.

INDEX

Malkerns Church 119
Malkerns Country Club 118
Malkerns Wine, Malt and Beer 118
Mall, the 63
Malolotja Environmental Education Centre
142
Malolotja Falls 142
Malolotja Nature Reserve 141, 142–143
Maloma 85, 89
Maloma Central Store 89
Mamphlo Grocery 128
Mananga 19, 136, 157
Mananga Agricultural Training Centre 160
Mangcongco Store 109
Mangelda Central School 157
Mangozeni Restaurant 118
Manica Travel Service 37
Mankayane 103, 104–105
Mankayane Hospital 105
Mankayane Park 105
Mankayane Supply Store 104
Mantabeni General Dealer 115
Mantenga Bottle Store 70
Mantenga Craft 43, 66, 76
Mantenga Falls 76, 77
Mantenga Falls Hotel 66, 75, 76, 77
Mantenga Foundation 76
Manzini 11, 21, 36, 41, 65, 119, 120, 122–
125, 137, 154, 164
Manzini Club 56, 122, 124, 125
Map Studio 41
Maphatsindvuku Grocery 165
Maphiveni 160
Maps 40–42, 132
Maputo 5, 46, 132
Maputo river 11
Marco's Trattoria 62
Markets 61, 62, 65, 85, 88, 99, 123, 125,
147, 166
Martin's Bar and Disco 70
Masai plateau 47
Maseru 46
Masks 119
Massage 70
Master Cleaners 118
Matilankhatsa Supermarket 87
Matsamo 19, 150, 170
Matsanjeni Health Centre 87
Matsanjeni Restaurant 87
Matsapha 120, 121–122
Matsapha Airport 19, 28, 46, 52
Matsapha dam 67

Matsapha railway station 50, 121
Matsetsa Roadside Store 168
Mauritius 16
Mawelawela Grocery 94
Mayiwane Store 155
Mbabane 21, 36, 41, 60–66
Mbabane Boat Club 116
Mbabane Club 64, 65
Mbabane river 64, 65, 67
Mbabane Youth Centre 64
Mbandzeni, King 6
Mbeya 47
Mbulungwane 95
Mbuluzana river 164, 169
Mbuluzi river 141, 142, 161
Mbutini hills 11, 135
Mdzimba hills 37, 71
Media 29
Medical facilities 30, 73, 86, 88, 90, 95, 105,
110, 114, 125, 147, 155, 166, 167
Medical insurance 30
Meikles Mount 114, 115
Memitsi river 91
Mennonites 64
Meridien Bank 20
Messina 47
Mfelankhono General Dealer 170
Mgazini 103
Mgenule Motel 69
Mgobodzi river 153
Mhlambanyatsi 107, 112, 113–114
Mhlambanyatsi Home Industries 114
Mhlambanyatsi river 115
Mhlathuze river 86, 90
Mhlatuze Breeding Ranch 90
Mhlosheni 11, 101
Mhlosheni hills 86
Mhlosinga Nature Reserve 132
Mhlume 133, 160
Mhlume Sugar Company 159
Middelburg 48
Midlands 10
Midway Store 70, 96
Military 84, 109, 160
Mineral springs 70
Mines 109, 135, 140, 141, 149
Minibus taxis 51–52, 93, 104, 111, 122, 123,
130, 141, 147, 154, 160, 163, 166
Ministry of Tourism, Commerce and In-
dustry 17, 41
Mishiandi Café 153
Mist 67, 95, 112, 117, 148

SOUTH
AFRICA

Josefsdal
Bulembu
P
EM
1

MALOLOTJA
NATURE RESURV

Enkhaba
Forbes Reef

Oshoek
Ngwenya
Motshane
Mbabane
MDZIMBA
1 494

Waverley
Lundzi
MLILWANE
WILDLIFE SANCTUARY
Ezulwini

Mhlambanyatsi
Lobamba
Kwa

Nerston
Sandlane
Bhunya
Matsap
Malkerns
Loyengo

MBULUNGENI
HILLS
Mankayane
Sidv

LAPANDA
1 382
Lusutfu

MAHLANGATS
HILLS

Sicunusa

Houdkop
HLABENIKOP
1 387
Grand

Bothashoop
Gege
LAGUBU
1 294

Mahamba
MOZAAN KOP
1 171
Nhlangand

Dwaleni

SWAZILAND REFERENCE

– – – – – –	International boundary
——	Main road
– – – – – –	Secondary road
〰〰	River
✚	Hospital
❶	Information bureau
⊠	Post office
⌡	Golf course
⚑	Border control post
⤬	Customs post
✈	Airfield
⊕	Clinic
▲	Places of interest
🚌	Bus terminal
Ⓟ	Police station